INVISIBLE NETWORKS
EXPLORING THE HISTORY OF
LOCAL UTILITIES AND
PUBLIC WORKS

Exploring Community History Series Editors

David E. Kyvig
Myron A. Marty

Invisible Networks

Exploring the History of Local Utilities and Public Works

Ann Durkin Keating

KRIEGER PUBLISHING COMPANY
MALABAR, FLORIDA
1994

Original Edition 1994

Printed and Published by
KRIEGER PUBLISHING COMPANY
KRIEGER DRIVE
MALABAR, FLORIDA 32950

FROM A DECLARATION OF PRINCIPLES JOINTLY ADOPTED BY A COMMITTEE OF THE AMERICAN BAR ASSOCIATION AND A COMMITTEE OF PUBLISHERS:

This publication is designed to provide accurate and authoritative information in regard to the subject matter covered. It is sold with the understanding that the publisher is not engaged in rendering legal, accounting, or other professional service. If legal advice or other expert assistance is required, the services of a competent professional person should be sought.

Library of Congress Cataloging-In-Publication Data

Keating, Ann Durkin.
    Invisible networks : exploring the history of local utilities and public works / Ann Durkin Keating.
        p.   cm. — (Exploring community history series)
    Includes bibliographical references and index.
    ISBN 0-89464-871-3
    1. Public works—United States—History.   2. Public utilities—United States—History.   3. United States—History, Local.
    4. Community.   I. Title.   II. Series.
    HD3885.K43   1994
    363'.0973—dc20   93-46988
                                                              CIP

10 9 8 7 6 5 4 3 2

CONTENTS

This 1917 view of Wall Street in New York City provides a glimpse of the invisible networks which make our modern life possible. *Courtesy of the Public Works Historical Society of the American Public Works Association, Kansas City, Missouri.*

EDITORS' INTRODUCTION

A sense of connection to a community of shared place, circumstance, or interest is an essential of personal well-being. Not to be attached to some community is to be isolated and adrift without either identity or security. Membership in a community offers an individual a sense of what is required of him or her, how to cope with situations confronted, and what to expect in the way of protection or punishment by conforming to or deviating from the norm. Community, in other words, makes it possible for humans to find their way in a chaotic and confusing world.

Communities exist in endless variety and contain a myriad of components. The traditional and most common image of community is the homogeneous village or town, but in modern mass society a community might be a compact, interactive neighborhood, an ethnic, religious, affinity, or professional group brought together by interest rather than geography, or a heterogeneous urban population sharing loyalties and experiences rather than direct personal contact. Today not only residents of Winesburg, Ohio, but those of East Harlem consider themselves a community, as do American and Canadian Ukrainians, Mormons, vegetarians, and dentists spread across the continent. Otherwise unconnected residents of Northeast Ohio unite as a community of sufferers for their professional sports teams just as Des Moines dwellers form a community of 1993 flood veterans. Whatever the nature and strength of the community, it is likely to contain or at least encounter a variety of institutions that carry out political, economic, social, educational, religious, cultural, or other functions that facilitate community life.

Communities are not instantaneous creations but the products of an evolutionary process. To appreciate the nature of a community, not to mention to function successfully in relation to it, requires an understanding of its development over time. Each community, given its distinctive identity, setting, and unfolding circumstances, possesses a unique past. Thus the task of recovering a community's history differs in every case. The discovery and analysis of an individual community's history can provide rewards to long-time members, newcomers, and outsiders alike, but will pose challenges to all.

Communities ought to know, and most instinctively do, that their own particular history is important to them. Recalling nothing of that past puts them in the same position as people suffering from amnesia, unable to remember their origins, their response to needs or challenges, their means of achieving success or dealing with setbacks, their sources of support or opposition, and their goals. History serves society much as memory serves an individual. In imperfect, sometimes distorted, but most often helpful fashion both help identify familiar elements in new situations and provide a guide to appropriate behavior. History also offers a standard of comparison across stretches of time and circumstance that exceed the span of an individual life. In this sense, history is far more than a remembrance of things past. History represents a means of coming to terms with the present, developing an awareness of previous influences, the continuities and distinctiveness in current conditions, and the range of future possibilities. Just as memory helps the individual avoid having to repeat the same discoveries, behaviors, and mistakes, historical knowledge helps a community, as well as any group or individual within it, avoid starting at the beginning each time an issue needs to be addressed.

Even if there is obvious value to a community in understanding its own history, the means of acquiring such self-knowledge are usually less evident, especially when the subject of interest is previously unexamined. Knowledge of the past is commonly gained from books, teachers, museums, films, or other presentations. What is one to do if the subject has never been explored, if there is no book on the topic in the library, if there is no expert to whom to turn? What is to be done in the even more likely circumstance that answers obtained from such sources are insufficient or unsatisfying?

A number of years ago, we began to appreciate that many people would like to explore the past of their own families and communities. Only the lack of research knowledge and confidence stood in their way. We realized from working with undergraduate students, local historical and genealogical societies, and out-of-school adults that any literate person motivated to explore some question regarding the past of his or her immediate surroundings could master most historical research methods, pursue most research possibilities, critically evaluate most potential explanations, and achieve a considerable measure of understanding. We felt it important to empower people to function as historians themselves or evaluate what others historians might say and write about a personally important past.

We began our effort to identify questions of historical significance and interest as well as explain how to investigate them in *Your Family History: A Handbook for Research and Writing* (Arlington Heights, Ill.: Harlan Davidson, 1978). Four years later we continued the undertaking with a larger book, one more widely focused on communities. *Nearby History: Exploring the Past around You* (Nashville: American Association for State and Local History, 1982) was, nevertheless, merely a general overview to a broad and complex subject. The warm reception which greeted *Your Family History* and *Nearby History* encouraged us to carry our notion further by providing specific advice on exploring particular topics. Enlisting historians who were experts on schools, homes, public places, places of worship, and businesses, we edited a five-volume Nearby History Series published by the American Association for State and Local History. We are now pleased to be able to expand the scope of these efforts through a series of books devoted to exploring community history that will be produced by the Krieger Publishing Company.

The inaugural volume in this series is Ann Durkin Keating's *Invisible Networks: Exploring the History of Local Utilities and Public Works*. It calls attention to the technologies that physically bind communities together, provides insight on their evolution, and suggests how their history can be investigated. Keating, a former research associate at the Public Works Historical Society as well as a highly regarded scholar of urban development, offers a fascinating and convincing demonstration of the importance of infrastructure to the development of the modern community. Through clear prose and vivid examples, she explains how water, power, waste, illumination, communication, and transportation systems have shaped the human environment. She also shows how historians can study these developments in the context of a particular community. Keating's innovative book should make evident that the study of utilities and public works is an essential element in the consideration of any community's past. In so doing, *Invisible Networks* will extend and improve the reconsideration of community history in a manner that will enrich community self-awareness and functioning.

DAVID E. KYVIG, Editor
MYRON A. MARTY, Consulting Editor

ACKNOWLEDGMENTS

Without the help of several individuals I would never have completed this book. Suellen M. Hoy's thoughtful and helpful comments challenged me to widen my discussion, as well as to improve my presentation. David E. Kyvig worked with this manuscript at every stage, and his suggestions improved the final version in many, many ways.

Howard Rosen and Joel Mendes of the Public Works Historical Society supported this project, especially with permissions, photographs, and archival material. I began this project as a staff member of the Public Works Historical Society, and this work is built on the nearly two decades of research and publications of that organization.

North Central College colleagues Jeffrey Charles, Pierre Lebeau, Barbara Sciacchitano, and Albert Welter provided their insights and support. I would also like to thank North Central College for a 1992 Summer Writing Grant, which aided in the completion of this book.

Finally, I would like to thank my husband John for his patience and encouragement, and our children Betsy and Jack for the joy they bring.

PART I

START WITH THE VISIBLE

Chapter 1

INTRODUCTION:
WHY EXPLORE THE
HISTORY OF PUBLIC WORKS?

We encounter public works everyday: turning on the water (or the television or the computer), flushing a toilet, flipping a light switch, waiting at a red light, sailing a boat, taking a train, making a phone call, waiting for an airplane, or crossing a river. Many times we are only aware of the ways in which we are dependent on public works when there are breakdowns: floods, potholes, power outages, collapsed bridges, or contaminated water.

In a very tangible way, public works are the sinews that make modern life possible. Without them, we are wilderness campers. We could not long survive in any but the smallest group without rudimentary public works. Disease, starvation, or other privations prevent humans from living together in communities without a water source, transportation for needed supplies, and a means of disposing of waste. Human beings have for millennia developed public works to allow themselves to congregate.

Pueblo, Colorado The need for public works in order to live in communities has existed for millenia. Nearly 1,000 years ago, the Pueblo Indians constructed an elaborate water system which made communal living possible in a naturally inhospitable area atop a narrow mesa in present-day southwestern Colorado. Erin S. Christensen and Gail L. Ukockis discuss what this water system meant to the Pueblo:

> Because of the labor expended on over 900 dams, and numerous reservoirs and ditches, it obviously represented an important contribution to the com-

3

munity. Faced with an arid climate, these people constructed check dams to help store irrigation water, reservoirs to supply domestic needs, and ditches to divert the vital liquid from one place to another. Because of the region's dryness, these facilities made human settlement viable. Domestic water stored in a particular reservoir, for instance, permitted a relatively large concentration of population to occupy the surrounding lands.

A humanly designed water system thus ensured a good quality of life, with fewer fears about nature's uncertainties. It also may have reinforced religious beliefs inasmuch as these Indians equated water with supernatural forces and traditionally used it in important ceremonies. Practically and spiritually this public works system enhanced the vitality of community life at Mesa Verde.

Source: Erin S. Christensen and Gail L. Ukockis, *Challenge to Build: A History of Public Works and APWA in Colorado*, James E. Hansen II, ed. (Fort Collins, CO: Colorado Chapter APWA, 1987):2.

Local historians of all backgrounds—whether they be members of local historical societies, academic historians, public works professionals, or independent researchers—find in infrastructure important information about the history of local communities. Researchers can use public works to define notions of community over time; to provide a base for understanding local government; to create a useful working tool for maintaining and understanding current structures; and to open an unusual window to everyday life in the past.

Local historians are students of communities over time. In a very real sense, a community can be defined as those individuals who willingly come together to create a public works. Obviously, there are overlapping communities within any single local area at any point in time—community can also be defined by things like church membership or school enrollment. However, public works provide a concrete indication of notions of community both today and in the past.

Public works history explains a great deal of the structure, organization, and functions of government within any community. There would be little need for village or city governments, without these communal projects. Because so much of the budget of any local government is consumed by infrastructure expenditures, understanding public works is critical to understanding local government and politics. Who pays and who receives services provides a key to power relationships within any community.

In addition, a knowledge of history is vital to maintaining and expanding current infrastructure systems. This history provides (or does not provide) important background information on the location and formation of projects which may not be visually obvious. For local historians interested in finding new areas of research, public works not only has intrinsic value, but helps engineers and local government officials to better understand the systems they operate.

Public works history also gives local historians insights into everyday life at points in the past. Through the lives of the builders of public works—laborers as well as engineers and politicians—local historians have a unique opportunity to explore the construction of their world. Examining this history also affords an opportunity to move inside households, to see how everyday life was transformed by various service connections. How was daily life, especially for women, changed by the introduction of these services?

Chicago, Illinois In April 1992, Chicagoans learned a great deal about local public works history when water came crashing into an old shipping tunnel system underneath the downtown area, flooding many stores and businesses. Work on pilings on the Chicago River earlier that spring had damaged a seal to a tunnel which intersected with the river.

This old system was virtually unknown to most Chicagoans. Nearly one hundred years ago, the Chicago Tunnel Company built the underground system as a way to alleviate traffic on busy downtown streets. The company bored through soft clay forty feet beneath the surface of the city and constructed sixty miles of tunnels connecting buildings in the downtown area. These tunnels eventually removed 5,000 delivery trucks from busy downtown streets. William Cronon explains that: "In addition, the tunnels became conduits for telephone cables. They carried pneumatic tubes, which served as the early twentieth century's equivalent of our fax machines. They even supplied skyscrapers with cool underground air as an early source of air conditioning."

By World War II, 3,000 freight cars and 117 locomotives shuttled goods around the downtown area. By the 1960s, delivery trucks had run the tunnel freight lines out of business. No longer used for shipping, the tunnel system only held communication cable lines. But in the days following the break, Chicagoans learned a great deal about tunnels underneath their buildings and streets, as efforts to reseal the tunnel entrance and pump out downtown basements (which often reached three or four floors below ground) received unusual media coverage.

Infrastructure history does not need to be so dramatic, but when it is in the public eye, it is often because of breaches such as the one in downtown Chicago in April 1992. As William Cronon notes: "As the flood so powerfully demonstrated, the perils of forgetfulness can be grave, and seem to be an increasing problem of modern life."

Source: William Cronon, "The Chicago Underground Flood of '92: Hidden Landscapes and Forgotten Perils in American Cities," *The New York Times*, May 2, 1992, Op-Ed Page.

Today public works are all around us and keep us going. But what are they specifically? Local historians may find it useful to focus on public works as physical structures and as processes. In addition, public works are variable over time and place.

The most basic way to look at public works is as physical structures. Suellen Hoy and Michael Robinson defined public works in their history of the subject: "The physical structures and facilities developed or acquired by public agencies to house governmental functions and provide water, waste disposal, power, transportation and similar services to facilitate the achievement of common social and economic objectives." This definition, then, includes many basic infrastructure systems: streets, water, waste disposal, gas, electricity, telephone, cable TV, and mass transportation. Public works also include prominent public structures with a variety of functions: post offices, city halls, courthouses, schools, parks, fire and police stations, lighthouses, train stations, and libraries.

Public works also encompass the planning, construction, and maintenance of the physical structures identified by Hoy and Robinson. Howard Rosen explains that public works include: "the design, construction, and maintenance of structures and facilities which government at all levels provides so that services essential to the functioning of organized society are available." Critical here is the role of local government. Exploring public works as processes draws local historians quickly into local government and politics.

Keep in mind, too, that public works do not comprise a static list of infrastructure and services. For the truth is, many of the functions listed as "public works" are now, or have been sometime in the past, provided by the private sector. And many services which we take for granted today were not a part of "public works" even one hundred years ago. Many municipalities stepped in to provide public support of new service systems when industrialization and modernization presented dramatic challenges to the health and safety of local residents.

Underground most communities in North America are systems of tunnels used for a variety of public works and utilities. In the nineteenth century, municipalities constructed elaborate brick sewer systems, some large enough for maintenance workers to move around with ease. In this photograph, the sewer is on the left and an overflow structure is on the right. *Courtesy of the Public Works Historical Society of the American Public Works Association, Kansas City, Missouri.*

Public works history is concerned with both physical structures and the people who build and maintain them. We can physically explore the landscape of public works—even if that would require digging down to tunnels and conduits. At the same time, communities of individuals build these projects. They are the products not of single individuals, but of groups of individuals working together. Governments provide the primary means by which groups plan, construct, and maintain public works. Their development and financing tell us a great deal about a community. The amount of public support needed to create an infrastructure system can be staggering, and the process of reaching consensus on such projects can reveal the innermost sensibilities of a community. The physical structures that make up public works, as well as methods of administration and financing, allow us a glimpse of what constituted the slippery concept of community, both today and at points in the past.

Kansas City, Missouri Beginning public works historians can turn to the knowledgeable help of the Public Works Historical Society. The Public Works Historical Society is the only organization dedicated to recognizing and documenting the historical achievements of the public works profession. Founded in 1975, today the Public Works Historical Society has over 1,800 members. It is a part of the American Public Works Association, and most of its members are professionals in the field of public works, with around 300 historians. The society provides its membership with a bimonthly newsletter filled with information about public works history, an annual oral history with an important figure in the field, and a series of essays in public works history. The Public Works Historical Society serves as a clearinghouse for information on public works history, for the use of professionals, historians, and interested laypeople. For more information about the Public Works Historical Society: 106 W. 11th Street, Kansas City, MO 64105-1806; (816) 472-6100.

Public works also take local historians beyond specific communities. There are a whole class of projects—often including dams, bridges, highways, and aqueducts—which are conceived, financed, and administered by a governmental body beyond an individual neighborhood or region. Thus, public works history moves the local historian to consider national (and even international) contexts.

Finally, while public works are primarily the product of communities, many of the systems are used within individual homes and businesses. Exploring the history of the connections between individual homes or businesses permits us to look at the dramatic changes which have taken place in everyday life over time. Just one hundred years ago, water and waste disposal were frequently individual responsibili-

Not only have the sorts of public works and utilities changed, but the work involved in the construction and maintenance of structures and systems has also evolved over time. Until well into the twentieth century, horses powered most construction equipment. The introduction of the automobile and truck reshaped public works equipment. Here, workers drive horse-drawn graders as a first step toward building new roads in Chicago. *Courtesy of the Public Works Historical Society of the American Public Works Association, Kansas City, Missouri.*

ties, with outhouses and backyard pumps the rule. Homes were poorly heated and lit by fireplaces, candles, and lamps that required no outside networks for their operation. Surely our lives have changed!

There are clearly several different vantages from which to explore the history of public works. This book will begin by examining structures within specific communities, to introduce the kinds of facilities that are identifiable as public works. Then the basic tools available to local historians will be identified. Armed with this information, the second part of the book will examine both infrastructure networks that tie homes to a community and networks that tie a community to a region. A final section will examine some of the more interesting ways in which infrastructure networks inform local history. Throughout, the role of government, changing notions of community and basic services, and the utilitarian uses for public works history will be emphasized.

Using public works to inform history is a task which local historians and more specialized public works historians have only begun to tackle. Creating the larger picture of public works history in the United States, Canada, and the rest of the world can only be done based on careful work in individual communities. A decade ago, Suellen Hoy identified many of the important questions which local historians could explore in the context of public works. While many of these subjects have begun to receive attention by some local historians, many are yet unaddressed:

> While it is known that municipal engineers were influential in initiating and implementing many reforms, what has not been documented is the precise nature of the relationship between the experts—engineers, landscape architects and health officials—and reform groups and politicians in local communities; nor is very much known about the sanitary policies of municipal, county and state governments. What determined the location of dumping sites on land and in water? When, where, and why were reduction plants and incineration facilities built? What were the reasons for the expanded efforts to purify water and build large filtration plants following World War I? And, since 1945, what has characterized the relationship between cities, counties and states and the federal government regarding the issues of waste disposal and wastewater treatment?

> Besides questions related to sanitary reform, there are many others that beg for answers. For example, what has been the role of the real estate industry in the community building process and the relationship between land values and public works? Almost nothing is known about the large-scale rec-

lamation projects undertaken by cities and counties after 1850. What impact did the construction of levees and the filling in of shorelines have on real estate and industrial growth? And, in large cities, how did promises of sewer and water systems affect annexation campaigns and the subsequent growth of suburbs? How did racial factors influence the location of critical public works, particularly in the rebuilding of towns and cities in the South following the Civil War? In the 20th century, to what extent were freeways and expressways routed through inner-city neighborhoods, and how did these routings change land use and commercial patterns? Did the placement of parks and recreational facilities affect land values? What elements determined the number and kinds of parks built by park districts, and what role did commissioners, neighborhood associations, and realtors play in the decision-making process? And, finally, what has been the effect of military bases and airports on local economies and values?

Source: From "Untapped History: A Public Works Historian Calls for a Closer Look at America's Infrastructure," *History News* 37:7 (July 1983):13–14.

SUGGESTED READINGS

The basic text in the public works history of the United States was published in 1976, as part of a Bicentennial project of the American Public Works Association. Edited by Suellen M. Hoy, Michael C. Robinson, and Ellis L. Armstrong, *History of Public Works in the United States, 1776–1976* (Chicago: American Public Works Association, 1976) provides basic information on the development of public infrastructure in the United States arranged in chapters considering different types of infrastructure such as water, sewers and wastewater treatment, roads, and bridges. Each chapter also includes a useful bibliography for further research.

Suellen M. Hoy and Michael C. Robinson compiled and edited *Public Works History in the United States: A Guide to the Literature* (Nashville: The American Association for State and Local History, 1982) as a companion volume to their history. This literature guide provides thousands of citations for further reading on various categories of public works: planning, irrigation, waterways, flood control, sewers, water, solid wastes, roads, mass transportation, airports, public buildings, parks, energy, and military installations.

In 1988, the Canadian Public Works Association sponsored the publication of a companion volume to the *History of Public Works in the United States. Building Canada: A History of Public Works* (Toronto: University of Toronto Press, 1988) provides essays on various categories of public works history in Canada, written by leading public works historians. The senior editor was Norman Ball, and Howard Rosen of the Public Works Historical Society served as the project director.

Together, these three volumes comprise a strong base for anyone interested in exploring public works history in North America. They provide important general information about the development of public works within which local infrastructure networks can be set. The Public Works Historical Society also publishes an essay series (as a benefit of membership) on specific topics in infrastructure history. These essays include discussions of: Fresno's water supply, Niagara Falls redevelopment, the Croton Aqueduct for New York City, and water and sewage works in Wilmington, Delaware. Particularly useful for its fine bibliographic essay is *Public Works and Urban History: Recent Trends and New Directions* by Eugene P. Moehring (Essays in Public Works History, Number 13, August 1982). Moehring focuses on the ways in which historians have explored infrastructure history in urban areas. For a complete listing of these essays, contact the Public Works Historical Society, 106 W. 11th Street, Kansas City, MO 64105-1806.

Other useful discussions are: Suellen Hoy, "Untapped History: A Public Works Historian Calls for a Closer Look at America's Infrastructure," *History News* 38:7 (July 1983); 12–14; and Josef W. Konvitz, *The Urban Millennium: The City-Building Process from the Early Middle Ages to the Present* (Carbondale, IL: Southern Illinois University Press, 1985). *Technology and the Rise of the Networked City in Europe and America*, edited by Joel Tarr and Gabriel Dupuy (Philadelphia: Temple University Press, 1988), is comprised of a series of essays by leading public works and urban historians on research in infrastructure history both in North America and in Europe. The volume provides an important comparative dimension between developments in North American and European communities. The book emphasizes the community base of most infrastructure networks, so is of particular interest to local historians interested in researching public works history.

Two succinct overviews of urban infrastructure development are: "Patterns in the Development of Urban Infrastructure" by Joel A. Tarr and Josef W. Konvitz in *American Urbanism: A Historiographical Review*, edited by Howard Gillette, Jr. and Zane L. Miller (New York: Greenwood Press, 1987); and Bruce Seely, "The Saga of American Infrastructure," *Wilson Quarterly* (Winter 1993): 19–39.

Chapter 2

EXPLORING VISIBLE NETWORKS: TAKING A SURVEY

Local historians have a major role to play in uncovering public works history. There are very few communities whose public works history has been carefully studied. Local historians have the skills and re- sources to add dramatically to our knowledge of public works.

Doing public works history, like many other aspects of local history, involves considerable archival investigation. But it also involves care- ful exploration of neighborhoods and structures. In fact, an excellent way to begin to explore the history of public works in any community is to take a walk or a drive through the area. Almost all public works have some sort of physical presence within a community, which can be ferreted out once you know what to look for. Most of the buildings or structures that you see around you on a casual walk or drive are either homes or businesses. In most instances, these are relatively easy to identify. Those structures remaining are the pool from which we can identify public works within a community.

Toronto, Ontario, is no exception to this general picture. Growing over the nineteenth century from a tiny town to an industrial center, Toronto is located on the western end of Lake Ontario with rail lines into a hinterland rich in agricultural and mineral products. Commu- nity residents constructed public works to aid in this growth and de- velopment. Let us turn for a moment to exploring those structures which are public works in Toronto.

Quite possibly the oldest extant public work in Toronto is Fort York. Like many communities in North America, the earliest European set- tlement concentrated in and around a military post, Fort York. An- other early public work found in Toronto is a public market. The St. Lawrence Market served as both a market and as the second city hall from its construction in the 1840s. Other structures of note are the current city hall, the Ontario Legislature building, the University of Toronto, Toronto General Hospital, and Osgoode Hall (home of the Provincial Court System).

All of these buildings share certain characteristics: they are public works because they are owned and operated by government, and they each house some governmental function. Other basic facilities include: schools, firehouses, and police stations. In virtually every community across North America there are public buildings such as these, and they form the core of visible public works.

Related to public buildings is another whole area of public works: parks and recreational facilities. In Toronto, one of the most striking recreational structures is the Skydome, opened in June 1989. The Skydome has a retractable roof, which opens or closes in twenty minutes. Other recreational facilities across Toronto include parks, playgrounds, marinas, pools, and footpaths. Again, the specific package of recreational facilities will vary from community to community, but seldom has a community chosen not to develop this area of public works.

Toronto, Ontario Once a physical survey is underway, research can begin on the history of significant structures. Among the pieces of information which a local historian will want to undercover are: events leading to construction, the construction itself, and the current status. Government is especially important to this—as the agent for these actions. Local historians will find in these explorations that local government is not simply a group of offices and politicians in a civic center, but a remarkable variety of structures which comprise the public works surveys.

In Toronto, many of the structures uncovered in a physical survey are under the supervision of the Works Commission of Metropolitan Toronto. Until 1956, thirteen municipalities independently constructed and managed public works structures in and around Toronto. Then, a new government entity, Metropolitan Toronto, took control of all government functions in the region. Toronto residents chose this new umbrella government to coordinate services in their rapidly expanding metropolitan area. The Works Commission of Metropolitan Toronto was a new agency, but it inherited old facilities, staff, and indebtedness.

Ross L. Clark, who was Works Commissioner from 1956 to 1979, was responsible for integrating many of the public works systems. Clark was born and raised in Toronto, and devoted virtually all of his career to public service. As Works Commissioner, Clark supervised the integration of water supply, wastewater treatment, air pollution control, and solid waste disposal. He closed small sewage treatment plants, abandoned old wells, and filtration plants. In their place, Clark supervised the construction of facilities whose capacities could serve the entire metropolitan area. As Howard Rosen explains: "Clark reigned as Works Commissioner at a time of transition from small-scale, fragmented organizations to a more integrated and modern system of public works. In addition to his technical competence, it was the personality of Ross Clark which enabled him to deal effectively with the complex and difficult adjustments that attended the amalgamation of thirteen heretofore independent jurisdictions. It was a bold, successful experiment which was not easily duplicated."

Source: Howard Rosen, "Ross L. Clark—Pioneer Metro Commissioner," *APWA Reporter* (April 1983): 10–11.

Another whole category of public works in evidence in Toronto is related to transportation. Toronto's early prominence was due to its position as a port—and today the Ferry Dock and the Toronto Harbour Commission Building serve as a reminder of massive projects undertaken to improve the harbor. For instance, during the 1920s a large landfill project filled in the lakeshore to create a new harbor area. A landfill project is an excellent example of another sort of imprint that public works leave on a landscape, reminding us that not all public works are buildings or structures. Is your community on a lake or river? In what ways has your community used and/or shaped this resource over the course of history?

By the middle of the nineteenth century, a new form of transportation had emerged: the railroad. The many, many miles of track still in existence are a visible reminder of the predominance of the railroad in Toronto. Another reminder is the colonnaded Union Station opened in 1927 under the combined direction of the City, the Harbour Commission, the railways, and the federal government. Railroad stations (and railway lines themselves) are excellent examples of projects which may or may not be considered public works: some are publicly controlled, while others remain in private hands. They point up the blurred distinction between public and private control of these facilities.

Other very important public works visible in and around Toronto and other communities are streets and highways. Prominent among the highways in Toronto are the Don Valley Parkway, the Gardiner Expressway, Highway 427, and Highway 401. Today community residents drive automobiles along these highways, but streets initially served residents on foot, on bicycles, on horseback, or in streetcars. In Toronto, there is a physical vestige of the streetcar age: one remaining building from a complex of structures that housed the Toronto Railway Company. Constructed in 1881, this building served as a stable for the 400 horses used to pull the streetcars. The structure now houses the Young People's Theatre. In other communities, these kinds of structures or stretches of track may serve as a reminder of a bygone age.

During the twentieth century, Toronto residents funded two additional public works devoted to transportation: the Yonge Street subway and the Island Airport. Along with highway construction, they constitute the more familiar transportation modes. If you walked or drove through Toronto, you would also encounter another public work vital to easy transportation: bridges. One particularly fruitful walk to explore bridges in Toronto is in the Don Valley, where concrete and steel bridges are readily apparent. In many communities, bridges are a critical public work in linking residents to the wider world.

Toronto, Ontario Behind bridges, or other public works structures, lies the work of engineers. For instance, engineer Thomas Taylor combined both expertise at bridge building and long-range planning in the design and construction of the Bloor Viaduct (across the Don Valley) between 1915 and 1918. Taylor, an engineer in the Railway and Bridge Division in the Toronto Department of Works, began his career with the Canada Foundry Company, where he designed and estimated steelwork for buildings. In 1912, Taylor worked with a team of engineers and architects to design two bridges, with room for a subway as well as vehicular traffic.

As Phyllis Rose explains: "Taylor was responsible for ensuring that this massive structure made an aesthetic as well as utilitarian contribution to Toronto. In addition, Taylor's efforts were also directed to building for tomorrow. Fifty years after the completion of this viaduct, the Toronto Transit Commission used the lower level for a subway line, a purpose Taylor anticipated in his original design."

Source: Phyllis Rose, "People in Public Works—Thomas Taylor," *APWA Reporter* (December 1987): 4–5.

Up until now, most of the functions of the structures found in Toronto and other communities have been readily apparent. Let's turn to some of the more unusual public works structures, whose purposes may not be clear. If you drove along the lakeshore in the Toronto neighborhood known as the Beaches, you would encounter a long low building of massive proportions. This is not a building generally open to the public, but it is a public work: the R. C. Harris Water Treatment Plant. During the 1930s, Toronto residents funded a massive project to improve the city's water supply. The treatment plant is only the most visible part of a project that included a rock tunnel two miles out into Lake Ontario, a supply tunnel seventy feet below street level for ten miles, and a number of reservoirs.

Toronto, Ontario Another way to explore the history behind the survey of any community is to research the name of specific structures. Often, the individuals whose names grace these buildings played a significant role in local history. While a survey is centered around physical structures, individuals shaped their construction.

For instance, the R. C. Harris Water Treatment Plant bears the name of Toronto's Commissioner of Public Works from 1912 to 1945. A *Toronto Telegram* tribute to Harris on his death in 1945 noted that "It is not stretching the truth to say that in the last quarter century, Mr. Harris exercised a greater influence on civic policies than most mayors and members of council." An editorial written by the *Toronto Star*, on the occasion of Harris's twenty-fifth anniversary as commissioner noted that:

> He had been works commissioner during the decades of road-building and bridge-building which followed the extensive pre-war (World War I) annexations to Toronto. Upon him, more than any other civic official, fell the burden of supplying these great annexes, as well as the older parts of the city, with modern municipal services. He brought to this task an integrity of purpose and skill in the handling of difficult situations. He has been the guide and counsellor of many colleagues at city hall. New aldermen and new officials have found in him a wise advisor and a real friend.

Harris devoted considerable time to meeting the demands of automobile traffic in Toronto by widening streets, building bridges, and working to alleviate downtown congestion.

One of Harris' projects, of which he was particularly proud, was the construction of the filtration complex at Victoria Park (R. C. Harris Filtration Plant). The plant, built between 1937 and 1941, provided for one of the largest water systems in North America. Its interiors were sumptously finished in bronze and marble, leading to its nickname "Palace of Purification."

Source: Howard Rosen, "People in Public Works—R. C. Harris," *APWA Reporter* (December 1982): 4–5.

Water supply is a key public works function. Most of us only think about the familiar final destination of water—taps within our homes and businesses—but there is a massive infrastructure behind these taps. Along with supply tunnels and filtration plants, another key building which is clearly visible (but may not be clearly identifiable) in many communities is the water pumping station. Toronto has a number—one is located just southeast of the Skydome. The John Street Pumping Station was built at the same time as the Skydome, but it is the third pumping station to be located on this same site since the nineteenth century. Reservoirs are located in many communities and Toronto has several. In 1894, one Toronto resident described the Rosehill Reservoir in this way: "The present waterworks are beautifully situated on a hill north of Toronto where a miniature lake of nine acres floored and walled with stone serves as a reservoir. The grounds are beautifully kept and overlook Mount Pleasant Cemetery." (Rose, p. 19) In other communities, water towers—elevated reservoirs—may be the most visible public works structure. Does your community have a reservoir system? When was it developed? Why?

Water is also behind another kind of public works project—those aimed at controlling floods and water damage. In many communities dams and flood plains are vital public works which protect the lives and property of community residents. Levees, dikes, and retaining walls also serve to protect residents from flood waters. In Toronto, the G. Ross Lord Dam is administered by the Metropolitan Toronto and Region Conservatory Authority and is a part of flood control efforts in the metropolitan area. Often flood plain areas are turned into park lands, with few structures that could be damaged in a heavy storm. In Toronto, the threat of flooding has led to the creation of a variety of public works. In other communities, the lack of water leads to the creation of public works. Extensive irrigation systems and water channels bring water from outside communities, allowing for settlement in otherwise arid regions.

Nor are buildings housing sewage treatment and disposal, as well

Engineers have played a critical role in the design, construction, and maintenance of public works and utilities across North America. Local historians often encounter their names on structures within their communities. Photographs of the public officials involved in construction projects are often found in local newspapers (after World War II), and in project files located in government offices. Here R. C. Harris (second from the right) is seen with other officials at the launching of an inspection scow in Toronto in 1913. *Courtesy of the Public Works Historical Society of the American Public Works Association, Kansas City, Missouri.*

as more general waste disposal, readily identifiable. In Toronto, there are four sewage treatment plants; the largest, familiarly known as Ashbridge's Bay, covers an area of approximately one hundred acres. In many municipalities, incinerators once burned garbage. Most are not in use today, but some remain standing—either empty or converted to other purposes. In Toronto, public works officials have converted one incinerator site into a collection depot for hazardous household waste. Other sorts of buildings found in many communities include transfer stations, where solid waste collected from curbside pickup is moved to larger vehicles before being transferred to landfill sites.

While the function of the communications tower atop the CN Tower in Toronto (the world's tallest free-standing structure) is easily discernible, other structures providing power and communication in-

frastructure are not as obvious. Electric generating stations and sub-
stations often are hidden behind facades which give little indication
of their use. In Toronto, the Richard L. Hearn Generating Station near
the lakeshore has stood unused for many years, adding to its mystery.

While a current survey of Toronto provides a great deal of information about public works, information about scenes which no longer
exist would enhance the public works dimension of the history of any
community. Local historians, with ready access to past descriptions of
their communities, can identify buildings or structures no longer
standing. Much of this work can be accomplished through a combination of physical survey and historical photographs.

Pullman in the 1880s, then on the outskirts of Chicago and today a
neighborhood within the city, provides an example of this expanded
public works survey—including both current and historical structures. Combining a physical survey with archival materials allows the
local historian to reconstruct a public works survey for some point in
the past. Pullman in the 1880s provides a setting for exploring an earlier period of public works within a specific community.

Pullman in the 1880s differed dramatically from Toronto today.
First, it was only a small part of a metropolitan area. Instead of large-
scale projects, a survey turns up small structures, with a closer connection to homes and businesses. Second, Pullman does not represent
a distinct local government. Today it is subsumed in various districts,
including the City of Chicago. In the 1880s, it operated largely independent of local government. Third, Pullman in the 1880s exhibited
the important role which private development of services has had on
some communities.

In the late 1870s, George Pullman, manufacturer of sleeping cars for
railroads, decided to build a factory and community on farmland to
the south of Chicago. Later, Pullman explained his motivations to the
United States Strike Commission:

> We decided to build, in close proximity to the shops, homes for working
> men of such character and surrounding as would prove so attractive as
> to cause the best class of mechanics to seek that place for employment
> in preference to others. We also desired to establish the place on such a
> basis as would exclude all baneful influences, believing that such a pol-
> icy would result in the greatest measure of success from a commercial
> point of view.

While the planners of Pullman envisioned a self-contained community, they had little sense of city growth and little control over it. Envisioned as a distinct, separate town, Pullman was engulfed both

Pullman, Illinois, was a company town located on the outskirts of Chicago. The Pullman Company, makers (and repairers) of sleeping cars, constructed the town in the early 1880s. The company not only built its manufacturing structures, but homes for managers and workers, office and commercial spaces, a market, a hotel, and a wide range of public works and utilities. The Pullman Company built and maintained these services until the turn of the century. This photograph includes the Administration Building of the Pullman Company, with Lake Vista in the foreground and the company water tower in the background. *Credit: Chicago Historical Society, ICHI-23065.*

physically and politically by the City of Chicago by the turn of the twentieth century. What had once been a separate place grew to be a neighborhood within a larger whole.

All improvements that today we identify as public works initially were made privately by the Pullman Company. The community of Pullman was located in the southern section of Hyde Park Township, but maintained a careful distance from this government. One contemporary source described: "The car company assumed many of the functions usually held by a city corporation. It furnished the residences with water, gas, and electric light. The streets of the town had never been dedicated to the public, and no plat of the town has ever been filed for record with the county authorities. To all intents and purposes, the Town of Pullman is still an acre tract." All Hyde Park provided Pullman was the use of its courts and jailhouse, and the service of two policemen. In 1882, the town also provided George Pullman with water, which he turned around and sold to his residents.

As mentioned above for Toronto, public markets and government centers often are among the earliest public works in a community. In Pullman, they were privately developed.

At the heart of Pullman today is a vacant lot. In the 1880s, there stood the Arcade Building, a block long and ninety feet high, the center of community life. A huge glass and iron arcade ran from front to back. A reporter in the 1880s found it a roofed-in American "oriental bazaar." The ground floor contained a dry goods store, pharmacy, tailor, and book store; the second floor had a billiard parlor, barber shop, meeting rooms, library, theatre, and offices of professionals and town officials. In 1883, a bank and a post office were added.

In an important sense, this building served as the town hall, although it represented private interests, rather than public ones. In the years before Pullman was annexed to Chicago, the one Hyde Park Board member who represented Pullman had his offices here, and he was always an executive from the Pullman Company.

The town agent, who was the Pullman Company officer in charge of the residential area, also had his offices in the Arcade Building. The town agent supervised the several departments that maintained streets and buildings, operated gas and water works, and offered fire protection. The town agent was also responsible for various business enterprises, such as the sewage farm. It was here that problems with water or sewerage or other services were handled, not at the Hyde Park Town Hall or the City Hall in Chicago after annexation in 1889.

The Pullman Company also constructed and maintained the market facilities for the community. The Market Hall still stands in Pull-

The Arcade Building in Pullman held offices for the Pullman Company, a library, offices, and other retail stores. *Credit: Chicago Historical Society, ICH-01888.*

man. The company leased the space to grocers and butchers. In the 1880s, it was the only place in the area for workers and their families to purchase food.

As a reporter for the *New York Sun* explained in 1883: "A stranger arriving at Pullman puts up at a hotel managed by one of Mr. Pullman's employees, visits a theatre where all the attendants are in Mr. Pullman's service, drinks water and burns gas which Mr. Pullman's water and gas works supply . . . visits a school in which the children of Mr. Pullman's employees are taught by other employees, and at night he is guarded by a fire department every member of which from the chief down is in Mr. Pullman's service."

Parks were also developed not by a public body, but by the Pullman Company in the early 1880s. Two parks remain from the era. Pullman Park, next to the Hotel Florence, originally fronted on a small lake and served as the "front yard" for the community. The company filled the lake in after 1898, when they began to sell off parcels in the community. Adjacent to the site of the Arcade is Arcade Park, with gardens and a bandbox. Parades and special events in Pullman in the 1880s often ended here. The Pullman Company also developed a recreational area directly to the east of the community on Lake Calumet. Boating, swimming, and fishing facilities all were provided by the paternalistic company.

In addition, the Pullman Company in the 1880s and 1890s improved and maintained streets and sidewalks, and provided both water and sewerage. Still visible in some parts of the community are parts of the original streets.

The most significant structure related to these services was a water tower (demolished in the early twentieth century), which also held sewage pumping facilities. For a short time after its construction in 1880, the water tower was the tallest structure in the world. The company purchased water directly from Hyde Park Township and then re-sold to it to residents. Nearby was a power house, which provided gas lighting to the whole of the town and industrial complex.

Chicago, Illinois Engineer Benezette Williams was a distinguished sanitarian, who worked with the Chicago water and sewer system in the decades previous to 1880, the year he was hired by the Pullman Company to design the water and sewer works. Williams was a civil engineer, who came to Chicago after graduating from the University of Michigan in

1869. By 1880, he had served as Chicago's superintendent of sewers, acting city engineer, and city engineer.

In 1880, George Pullman commissioned him to design and construct the water and sewer system of Pullman, Illinois. This was undoubtedly the assignment for which he is most remembered. Due to the swampy conditions, Williams had to drain and grade the land before construction. Williams installed pipes to run excess water into nearby Lake Calumet. Once the land was dry, Williams laid water, sewer, and gas mains.

After his work at Pullman, Williams returned to work for the City of Chicago. From 1892 to 1893, he served as the chief engineer of the Chicago Sanitary District. Before his death in 1914, Williams also designed sewer and water systems for St. Louis, Seattle, LaCrosse, Saginaw, Council Bluffs, Decatur, and many other smaller communities.

Source: Suellen Hoy, "People in Public Works—Benezette Williams," *APWA Reporter* (January 1981): 4–5.

Another site which historical photographs of Pullman uncover is the sewage farm. Today, it is beneath the Calumet Expressway. This is one of the few examples of a sewage farm which was actually put into use in the United States. Sewage from the town was piped to a treatment facility and then used to irrigate farms which raised produce which the company sold in the Market Hall.

The Pullman Company not only planned the town and built improvements, but also constructed housing for both management and workers in the adjoining carworks. Water, sewer, and gas connections were made by the company for housing as well as industrial and commercial sites. A survey today shows the various kinds of housing which the company constructed—from elegant mansions for top management to tenement houses for unskilled workers. The Pullman Company owned all housing, charging a monthly rent, along with extra charges for water, garbage collection, fire protection, and other services. When the housing was built in the early 1880s, even the tenement houses had what were considered modern conveniences—with one water tap per structure.

After Pullman was annexed to Chicago in 1889, water came to the town directly from the city, which upgraded its southside pumping station during these years, improving the supply of water to Pullman. However, the Pullman Company continued to resell the water to community residents, because the City of Chicago honored Pullman's water contract with Hyde Park until it expired in 1892. Then, Pullman Company executives began negotiations with Chicago officials who wanted higher water rates. Mayor John Hopkins, himself an embittered former Pullman employee, tried to increase the water rate charged the Pullman Company. At the same time, Hopkins sought to reduce the water fees which residents paid the Pullman Company. Hopkins was successful in raising the water rates paid by the Pullman Company, but residents continued to buy their water from the Pullman Company. (Hopkins also fought the Pullman Company to change the area's mailing address from Pullman to Chicago.)

This selective tour of public works in Pullman during the 1880s and Toronto in the 1990s should make clear the wide range of facilities that fall under the rubric of public works. A similar survey can be done for any other community, large or small—at any time in its history. Once you have an inventory of the sites, attention can be turned to questions of historical import. When were each of these public works developed? Why? What government body (or private company) created them? Who was involved in the decision-making process? Who benefitted from the development of the public work? Who paid for them? Who designed the structure or system? Who actually built the public work? Who has administered and maintained the project since its completion? How did this public work affect the daily lives of community residents? In what ways does this public work help us to understand the concept of community held by residents at any given point in time? The next chapter will provide some basic tools to begin to answer these questions.

SUGGESTED READINGS

The information on Toronto provided in this chapter was drawn from the tour book developed by the Ontario Chapters of the Canadian Public Works Association, *Exploring Public Works* by Phyllis Rose. Local chapters (and particularly chapter historians) of the American Public Works Association and the Canadian Public Works Association are a valuable source for information on local infrastructure networks. Contact the Public Works Historical Society, 106 W. 11th Street, Kansas City, MO 64105-1806.

Materials on Pullman are drawn primarily from two sources: William J. Adelman, *Touring Pullman: A Study in Company Paternalism* (Chicago: Illinois Labor History Society, 1977); and Stanley Buder,

Pullman: An Experiment in Industrial Order and Community Planning, 1880-1930 (New York: Oxford University Press, 1967).

It is worth contacting the public and private agencies that administer infrastructure networks in a community to see if any tours or descriptions have already been put together that provide historical information. For instance, the Metropolitan Water Reclamation District of Greater Chicago has a series of six tours of its facilities which include a powerhouse and several water reclamation plants. Tour information provides a base for further historical research.

Public agencies also occasionally publish their own histories. For instance, Fort Collins, Colorado, published a history of wastewater service in its community in 1988. Written by Erin Christensen and Karen Waddell, *How the Waste Was Won: A Century of Wastewater Service in Fort Collins* (Fort Collins, 1988) provides an account of the introduction and development of wastewater services in one community. Similar efforts have been made in other communities across North America, often in conjunction with special anniversary publications.

Chapter 3

BASIC TOOLS FOR EXPLORING PUBLIC WORKS HISTORY

Local historians exploring public works make important use of visual sources. Existing structures and facilities provide the first connection to the networks that provide basic local services. Photographs and other historical images allow local historians to identify structures that have been destroyed. Armed with a list of public works (both those demolished and those still standing), a local historian is ready to begin to ask basic questions about each of the structures: When was it built? What is it called (and why)? Under whose supervision? What kinds of labor and materials were needed in construction? What governmental body was involved? Is this the same governmental body that maintains the structure today? What is the structure used for?

Rome, Italy Public works have played a vital role in community history not just in recent generations, but for millenia. The ruins of Roman highways and aqueduct systems can be seen across Europe today. This visible evidence of historic systems provides modern-day historians with important visual evidence. Nowhere is this evidence more abundant than in Rome. As Howard Rosen explains:

At its height, Rome was inhabited by nearly two million people. It was the center of an empire that stretched from Britain, across Europe and North Africa, all the way to Afghanistan. Enforced by their legions, the Pax Romana (Roman peace) endured nearly five centuries—until 455 A.D. when the Vandals sacked the city.

All roads did lead to Rome. Under the Empire, 180,000 miles of paved roads were built, 53,000 of which were main highways. . . . Appius Claudius, a blind censor, built the famous Appian Way (300 B.C.), which opened up the

29

rich Campania to Roman trade. He was also responsible for the Aqua Appia, which provided the first water supply for the city. . . .

Some 200 [aqueducts] were built throughout the empire. There were 11 aqueducts for Rome, 10 to 60 miles in length. They brought in a constant supply of fresh water (and olive oil!). Giant cisterns provided Roman citizens with public baths, fountains, and drinking water. Using inverted siphons and lead pipes, many fortunate Romans had the unprecendented luxury of indoor plumbing. A sewer system, the Cloaca Maxima, carried wastes into the Tiber.

Source: Howard Rosen, "People in Public Works—Builders of Ancient Civilizations," *APWA Reporter.*

A useful first stop is the public works department. In some communities, there is no public works department. Instead departments may be organized along other lines: general services, works, streets and sanitation, transportation, water, or sewers. Basic information on at least some of the structures will come from these departments.

Of course, other governmental agencies may maintain many of the structures identified in a survey and through historical photographs. Schools, parks, dams, flood plains, highways, and bridges are often administered by separate agencies, which must be ferreted out by the local historian. To get a sense of the universe of governmental agencies, read the government section of the local phone book. In some communities, the League of Women Voters provides a guide to all governmental units. These may help in finding the agency which has responsibility for a particular structure or facility. Another useful starting place is a careful review of a local property tax bill, which often contains a breakdown of taxes into specific districts, agencies, and governmental units.

Sacramento, California The Sacramento Local Agency Formation Commission compiles a *Directory of Sacramento County Service Providers* at regular intervals. This directory provides an overview of all public service providers in Sacramento County, including: size and geographical service area; top administrators; historical and political data; and service and operational information. The fifth edition of this directory, published in 1986, includes over 200 pages of entries.

Among the categories of service providers listed are: air pollution control districts, cemetery districts, drainage districts, fire districts, garbage service providers, maintenance districts, mosquito abatement districts, multipurpose districts, electric company, park and recreation districts, a port district, reclamation districts, resource conservation districts, the Sacramento Municipal Utility District, sanitation districts, street lighting maintenance districts, and water purveyors.

A local historian interested in one particular community or neighborhood within Sacramento County could work through this directory and identify those units of government with responsibility for delivering services.

Also important to remember is that neither the physical survey or many lists from public agencies will identify facilities administered by private authorities. The local gas, electric, or telephone company provides important infrastructure for modern living, but none is strictly in the public sphere. Again, utilities are often listed in a special section of the phone book, and that may help get the search underway.

Along with uncovering information about structures identified in a survey of existing and historical structures, local historians can turn to written and oral sources to create a timeline of service introduction in their area. While to a certain extent, this task overlaps with the survey outlined in the previous chapter, a timeline helps to identify hidden networks which provide little or no visible marker of their presence. Some services rely on networks buried underground (water, sewer, and gas lines), while others revolve around equipment, not physical networks (garbage and snow removal). Such a timeline may include the initiation or construction of the following services and public works: town hall, fire and police headquarters, roads, public water, railroads, parks, telephone, gas and or electricity, sewers, garbage collection, parking lots, landfills, and public transit.

Lynnfield, Massachusetts Begin a basic timeline for public works for your community by examining published sources in local history. The following timeline for public works in Lynnfield, Massachusetts, a suburban community outside Boston, is drawn entirely from a local history.

Lynnfield Public Works Timeline

1680	Summer Street laid out as a king's highway
1814	Lynnfield becomes a separate incorporated town, with a population of around 100
1830s–1850s	Newburyport Turnpike operated through the town
1850	First passenger railroad service
1895	First long distance telephone wire
1902	Two-room school house, population over 1,000 First park
1908	Fire house construction begun
1913	First bus transportation initiated
1914	First paved road
1925	Central water system was established with the creation of the Lynnfield Water District
1957	Lynnfield Water District begins receiving water from the Metropolitan District Commission
1958	State highway bypass built
1959	End of passenger railroad service

The limits of relying solely on published local sources to reconstruct the public works history of a community are made clear by this example. Many services are not discussed, including: gas, telephone service, cable TV, sewer system, and early water service. Nor are these events necessarily related to physical structures or to governmental bodies. Yet, this sort of timeline is a useful place to begin a local public works history.

Source: Marcia Wilson Wiswall, ed., *Lynnfield: A Heritage Preserved, 1895–1976* (Lynnfield Heritage Associates, 1977).

A straightforward way for local historians to begin a timeline is to turn to published—or unpublished—community histories. Begin by examining the local history collection at the public library. Querying reference librarians often yields other useful materials that may be housed at a nearby historical society, university, archive, or public agency. The inauguration of public works is often a time of community celebration and is generally noted in local histories or newspapers. While this is by no means a systematic or error-free method of creating an initial list of community public works, it is a start. And perhaps as importantly, by working from the context of a more general local history, local historians can see the special role which public works have played within a community. This work does provide a base from which primary research in written, oral, and visual sources can begin.

Local historians have available to them some unusual sources. Physical artifacts from public works which have been destroyed provide important information about invisible networks. Many communities have public museums or private collections that contain artifacts. For instance, there are many transportation museums across North America. Many contain fine examples of streetcars, trolleys, railroad cars, and other vehicles. Local historical museums sometimes include antique streetlights, water pipe, wrought iron trim, and other materials that were once a part of public works within a community. In 1984, the North Carolina Museum of History organized an exhibit called "Public Works: Building a Better Life." This special exhibit brought together public works materials from communities across North Carolina. In areas with a public works project of major significance, there may be a related museum or exhibit adjacent to the facility. Many of the remaining lighthouses in North America operate as museums, providing information of local maritime and navigation history. Many are included in: F. Ross Holland, *Great American Lighthouses* (Washington, DC: Preservation Press, 1989).

Museums focussing on the recreation of historical communities sometimes display public works artifacts. For instance, at Old Salem, North Carolina, the focus is on the restored buildings of an early nineteenth century Moravian village. Included in the related museum exhibits are fragments of white oak water pipes used in the construction of the community's original system in 1778.

Occasionally, researchers uncover physical artifacts not yet housed in museums or archives. Researchers mights be rewarded by contacting local public works, street and highway, water, or sewer departments (or other pertinent government agencies), regarding old equipment and materials. Sometimes these agencies have warehouses that include obsolete parts to public works facilities. Also, whenever a construction project is undertaken, old street paving, sewers, and sidewalk materials may be unearthed. Local researchers should let construction crews know of their interest in old or obsolete materials and equipment.

Baltimore, Maryland Baltimore is one of the few communities in North America to have an entire museum dedicated to the history of its infrastructure. Opened in 1982 in a historic public works structure, the Eastern Avenue Pumping Station, the museum developed under the guidance of the Baltimore Department of Public Works. Curators collected photographs, manuscripts, and artifacts which could be used in exhibits and programs that explain the physical development of Baltimore, as well as the effect of this development on domestic and commercial life. Glass plate negatives, wooden water pipe, early asphalt paving equipment, old gaslights, and fireplugs are all on display at the museum.

Special exhibits at the museum over the past decade have included "Tapping New Sources: The Development of Baltimore's Water Supply," "Baltimore's Bridges and Their Builders," "The Livable City" (History of Sanitary Engineering), "Tunneling Beneath Baltimore," "Women in Public Works History," and "Taking the Lid Off Garbage: A History and a Challenge."

Museum visitors include area residents, school groups, and tourists. Many different organizations have contributed to the creation of each of the exhibits. All these activities and participants have revolved around the idea that public works are essential to the quality of life in an urban environment and that infrastructure makes cities not only possible but livable.

Photographs are among the most important visual sources available to local historians. Beginning in the middle of the nineteenth century, photographers began to capture not only completed public works projects, but those under construction as well. Aside from excavation work itself, there is perhaps no other source that allows us a truer glimpse of these "invisible networks." Collecting photographs for a local area provides an important source of information for public works and local history.

Construction photographs also highlight another important aspect of public works: the tremendous labor requirements of most projects, especially in the nineteenth and early twentieth centuries. Unskilled labor completed much of the back-breaking work of building massive facilities in communities across the country. Many of these laborers were immigrants, and their stories are largely untold. Local historians with an interest in the everyday people of their community can do groundbreaking work in this area. These workers, as well as the engineers who designed, supervised construction, and administered projects, are another important part of the public works story within any community.

Photographs are often located in local library or historical society

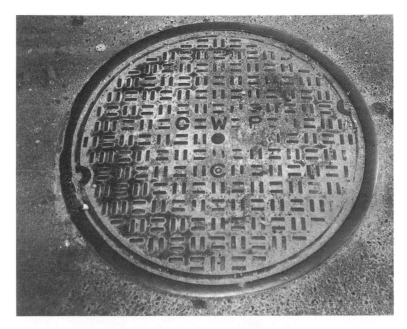

Research in public works history can begin by looking down at streets, sidewalks, and even manhole covers. These visual clues point to the systems often found beneath streets. Initials and dates on manhole covers can provide information about the agency that built a water or sewer system and the timing of the improvement. In many communities, manhole covers have interesting, and sometimes intricate, designs which add to the richness of the urban landscape. *Courtesy of the Public Works Historical Society of the American Public Works Association, Kansas City, Missouri.*

collections. Local government agencies also frequently maintain their own photograph files—both current and historical views. Other sources for public works photographs include state historic preservation agencies, state archives, the National Archives (particularly if the project is federally funded), and private photograph and postcard collections.

Wacounda, Illinois One fascinating source of historical images of public works and infrastructure improvements is postcards. In the years before mass-marketed magazines with photographs (the first two decades of the twentieth century in particular), postcards provided inexpensive images of structures and events within a community. Water towers, courthouses,

A-8473 Court House Park, Waukegan, Ill.

Before consumers had access to inexpensive cameras, postcards were a popular means of keeping a record of places visited and important events. Especially in the first several decades of the twentieth century, there were postcard views of important buildings and streets in communities across the country. This 1905 view is from a postcard printed by the Curt Teich Company of Chicago of the Court House Park in Waukegan, Illinois. *Courtesy of the Lake County Museum, Curt Teich Postcard Archives, Wauconda, Illinois.*

reservoirs, and downtown streets were stock scenes for postcards which were sold in local communities. In addition, natural disasters such as floods also made their way into postcards, preserving the historic event for residents and those they corresponded with.

One of the most spectacular collections of postcards from communities across North America is the Curt Teich Postcard Archives, a department of the Lake County Museum in the north suburban Chicago area. The materials now housed at the museum are composed of the industrial archives of the Curt Teich Company of Chicago, which operated from 1898 through 1974 as the world's largest volume printer of view and advertising postcards.

The materials at the Teich Archives are computer indexed by date, subject, and location. Views may be searched in any of these categories. Approximately 320,000 of the estimated 400,000 image records in the archives have been catalogued. A reproduction service is available through which photographic prints or transparencies may be ordered. Mail and telephone requests are encouraged; it is not necessary to visit the archives in order to use its holdings.

Source: The Curt Teich Postcard Archives, Lake County Museum, Lakewood Forest Preserve, Wauconda, IL 60084 (708)526-8638.

Other visual records, which are of critical importance to understanding the history of a public works facility, include several kinds of public records: maps of infrastructure systems, engineering blueprints, construction plans, and/or architectural renderings. Once a local historian has identified a structure for further investigation, finding these materials becomes vital to formulating a clear picture of the design and construction process. Files on public works structures still in use are often located with the agency charged with maintaining them. Obsolete structures or those that have been destroyed may be more difficult to track down. The local landmarks preservation agency may have materials on structures which have, or are being considered for, landmark status.

Calgary, Alberta The Calgary Engineering Department in 1977 published *The Bridges of Calgary, 1882–1977.* The book's origins lay in the fact that the city government received "several hundred calls a year from citizens wanting technical, general or historic information about various

SAN FRANCISCO-OAKLAND BAY BRIDGE, CALIFORNIA

PHOTO COURTESY SAN FRANCISCO EXAMINER

4A-H849

Postcards continue to provide important visual evidence of major public works projects. Here a postcard celebrates the dramatic view created by the San Francisco-Oakland Bay Bridge, California. *Courtesy of the Lake County Museum, Curt Teich Postcard Archives, Wauconda, Illinois.*

City Bridges. This book was designed and published to serve Public Libraries and the School Systems of Calgary as well as all Provincial Archives and to be available at cost to interested citizens." The book describes 65 representative bridges (from 148 total) for which the Calgary Engineering Department was then responsible. As well as providing historical background and technical data on each of the bridges, the volume includes many historical photographs and plans.

The Centre Street Bridge history is one of the longer entries:

The first crossing at Centre Street was Fogg's Ferry in 1882. Later a steel truss bridge, with wooden approaches, was privately built and operated as a toll crossing. The village of Crescent Heights petitioned for better access to downtown Calgary and the City Engineer obliged by building wooden steps on the slope from the base of the toll bridge up on 4th Street, N.W. In 1912, planner Thomas Mawson had been employed and proposed a grandiose level bridge complete with lagoons and a Mall terminating at the Canadian Pacific Railroad Station. At the north end he proposed a gigantic elevator or funicular railroad up the North Hill. After ascertaining costs, Council rejected his plans.

The private bridge could never meet its costs, fell into disrepair, and in 1911 it was offered the City for $7000 and it was repaired and put to use. In 1915 the bridge was condemmed for all but pedestrian traffic and it was sold to the Alberta Highways Departments for $1500 f.o.b. site in 1917.

During the June 1915 flood and whilst City Engineer Craig and his commissioners were inspecting it, the north wooden approach collapsed dumping them into the river. They were rescued by a handy rowboat at the Lagevin Bridge and Craig lost no time in finalizing construction of the present bridge.

The present concrete structure was started early in 1915 and officially opened in November 1916 with a big citizens parade led by Mayor M. C. Costello on foot. Early automobiles—especially the Model T Ford—had more power in reverse and many had to back up the 3.8% grade. The Bridge was completely renovated in 1974 and automatic land lights installed to permit maximum traffic flow at rush hours.

Source: Calgary Engineering Department, *The Bridges of Calgary, 1882–1977* (Calgary, 1977).

One excellent place to look for visual records is within written records of public agencies. Public works, water, street, or sanitation departments in many communities must submit annual reports on their activities. At some points in time and in some communities, these reports have been elaborate bound volumes, which include many of the blueprints, maps, and photographs that have been discussed above.

Annual reports from city, town, or village departments also include much basic information about public works within a community. Armed with the completion date of a facility within a community, a local historian can examine annual reports for the years in and around that date for information about construction, costs, and individuals involved in the process.

New York, New York Exploring the public works history of the City of New York is a complicated and complex task. Historian Eugene P. Moehring researched the history of public works in nineteenth-century New York. He worked with a wide variety of sources which provided information about the development and maintenance of infrastructure systems within the city which included: sewers, water lines, bridges, schools, fire and police departments, buildings, port improvements, and private utilities like gas and electricity.

Among the public documents which Moehring worked with were numerous published reports. Moehring consulted two series published by the New York City, Board of Aldermen: *Documents* (35 volumes, 1835–1870); and *Proceedings* (over 200 volumes for the same time period). From these bound volumes, Moehring was able to trace ordinances governing street improvements and other public works, as well as specific problems which city departments wrote reports about over the course of the nineteenth century. Also contained within the *Documents* were annual reports for many of the city departments, including those closely involved in public works. Moehring also utilized the published annual reports from a wide range of city agencies and departments, including: Board of Education, Central Park Commission, Croton Aqueduct Department, Department of Docks, Department of Police, Department of Public Works, Fire Department, and Board of Metropolitan Police.

Source: Eugene P. Moehring, "Public Works and the Patterns of Urban Real Estate Growth in Manhattan, 1835–1894" Ph.D. dissertation, City University of New York, 1976.

By turning to city, town, or village council meeting minutes (or appropriate committee meeting notes) from the years preceding the initiation of a project, more pertinent information is uncovered. The debate preceding the construction of a public work tells local historians a great deal about the motivations and needs of a community at a particular point in time. Such discussion also heightens awareness about the political and financial sides of public works projects. "Who gets and who pays?" are the key twin questions that council or committee meeting notes can help answer.

One of the best places to begin a search for council minutes is in the City (Village) Clerk's Office. More often than not, one of the mandates of this job is to serve as the official record-keeper for a municipality. Both published and unpublished minutes should be available for public perusal in most communities. They are used most effectively if a researcher is armed with some basic dates surrounding a project, as the minutes are invariably in chronological order (and are seldom, if ever, indexed). In some larger communities, a municipal reference library is charged with this portion of the City (Village) Clerk's job and it is to this agency that a researcher should address queries about historical materials.

Some local libraries also maintain a full run of all local government publications and open hearings and meetings. They are not always kept in a separate historical section, but may be grouped with current government publications and hearings.

Sometimes, local newspaper coverage of these council or committee meetings helps local historians to better understand the issues involved in the decision to build a public work. A newspaper may take an editorial stand either for or against a project, aiding historians in deciphering the past. In some communities, official records of town, village, or board meetings have been lost due to fire, flood, or some other natural or manmade disaster. Newspapers then are one of the few sources available to fill in the holes in the public record. Many local papers, particularly in the years before World War II, provided detailed minutes (and even occasionally verbatim transcripts) of public meetings.

Newspapers also provide an excellent way to track the construction of a project. From newspaper accounts, a researcher can track: the origins of the project; initial decisions about financing and construction; the public agency and/or the firm(s) involved in the construction; construction contracts; employment opportunities created by the project (possibly through employment advertisements); status reports on construction; and information about completion and dedication of a project.

Wheaton, Illinois In 1891, Wheaton, a small community located thirty-odd miles west of downtown Chicago along the Northwestern Railroad, was in the midst of a public debate about water supply. A letter to the editor from a prominent Wheaton resident, J. Q. Adams, helps historians in understanding the issues:

> Mr. Editor: It is not for the sake of notoriety, or to sharpen the edge of some ax of my own that I again trespass upon your valuable space, to urge upon my fellow citizens of Wheaton the necessity of inducing the City Council to immediately initiate the project of city waterworks. I am merely trying to secure what I know will be for the best interest of our city. I have no faction to please or injure. I seek the good of all.
>
> There are men in every place, and Wheaton is no exception, who like to own property and have their neighbors pay for all that really goes to improve the town. They want a few to be constantly going down into their pockets to benefit others who are able, but unwilling to ever make any progress, or improvement in their surroundings—if they have to pay their fair share. . . . .
>
> Let us follow the lead of other progressive places like Norwood Park, Elmhurst, Tuscola—all bonded for waterworks—and manfully pay for what we so much need. We need the water supply now. Then let the city fathers take immediate steps for securing what is so very necessary for our health, comfort, and protection, and for the construction of which the law provides an economical way.

Source: "The Water Question," *Wheaton Illinoian*, October 2, 1891, p. 1.

Exploring the lives of key individuals involved in the creation of a public works facility can be accomplished through a series of written sources. Engineering journals and societies provide a good place to find biographical materials on engineers who designed major public works projects. Local biographical files, often located at the public library, will aid in tracking down information on more locally based engineers and political officials. Many of these individuals were members of the local elite, and records of commercial or cultural clubs may also provide biographical information. If a historian can establish the date of death of an individual, local newspaper obituaries provide key information about careers. Published memoirs and autobiographies are fine sources—when they are available. Unpublished diaries and reminiscences can also provide information about the role of individuals in the creation of public works.

Public works projects affected not only the lives of engineers, but also laborers because these projects created many, many jobs within a community. What kinds of jobs were available and who got these jobs are questions which can be answered looking not only at the kinds of sources discussed above, but also to memoirs and diaries of local community residents of the construction era.

Public works departments also sometimes keep lists of employees within project files—these can be a gold mine for a public works historian interested in exploring those whose labor created a project. The role of minority and immigrant workers on public works projects is an important, and as yet, little explored area.

Chicago, Illinois The role of women in the creation of public works is an area little explored by historians. Research into the contributions which women have made to public works history is very much needed.

One woman whose contribution has been identified is Mary McDowell, who was known to many Chicagoans as "the Garbage Lady." McDowell was one of a group of women in communities across the country who took up the task of improving the urban environment in the late nineteenth and early twentieth centuries. As the director of the University of Chicago settlement house in the packinghouse district of the city at the turn of the last century, McDowell witnessed firsthand the environmental hazards which the stockyards created. Suellen Hoy describes the area surrounding the settlement house:

> The neighborhood was bound on the east by slaughterhouses; on the west by city garbage dumps; and on the north by "Bubbly Creek," a dead arm of the Chicago River covered with a thick scum through which carbonic gas occasionally oozed. . . . [McDowell] was continually annoyed by the unpleasant odors emanating from nearby slaughterhouses, vacant lots adjacent to them that were used as "hairfields" (where hair disposed of by the slaughterhouses putrefied in the process of drying), garbage dumps, and "Bubbly Creek."

McDowell came to the conclusion that "women must come to regard their city as their home" and that "home must not end with the front doorstep." She spoke to groups all around the city and organized a waste committee which focussed its attention on refuse waste disposal. McDowell was instrumental in the construction of a small incineration plant in Packingtown to reduce garbage. With the elimination of neighborhood dumps, the death rate in the neighborhood dropped.

Source: Suellen M. Hoy, "People in Public Works—Mary McDowell," *APWA Reporter* (September 1979):4–5, 19.

Before garbage collection became a municipal function, private scavengers often roamed through streets and alleys. Precursors of modern recycling, these scavengers made a living by collecting and selling anything from tin cans to paper scraps. Sometimes even pigs and other animals ranged around in the garbage. In the late nineteenth century, municipalities began to provide regular garbage collection and street cleaning. *Courtesy of the Public Works Historical Society of the American Public Works Association, Kansas City, Missouri.*

Of course, if a public works project was completed in the last several decades, it may be possible to interview the men and women who were involved in the planning and construction process. Armed with basic information about a project, an interviewer can often learn much that is in no written source from this sort of project. Often, a useful place to begin is with current employees of the public works (or related) department. Both highly placed individuals, as well as those in more modest positions, may provide valuable information about projects which were undertaken during their tenure with the public agency.

It is often easiest to tape oral interviews, and transcripts of these interviews (or the tapes themselves) become new local history sources. Be sure to gather basic information about the interviewer and the interviewee, as well as the date of the interview. Questions which would help provide basic information about a public works project include:

What is your background and training? What sorts of public works projects have you worked on over the course of your career? Did you work on the XXXX project? What was a typical day like during the construction? How did the community respond to the project, the construction? What kinds of equipment were used? How many people worked on the project? Did many workers come from within the community (or from outside)? What are the names of some other people who might be able to provide more information on a particular project?

Los Angeles, California Donald C. Tillman headed many of the public works efforts that met and anticipated the tremendous growth of the City of Los Angeles since World War II. In a public career that spanned five decades, Tillman worked in public works, as President of the Board of Public Works and as City Engineer. He was interviewed in August 1989 for an article in the *APWA Reporter,* the monthly magazine of the American Public Works Association. In the interview Tillman discussed the most important infrastructure project of the post–World War II period in Los Angeles:

> . . . It was that very freeway system that held me with Los Angeles. Los Angeles was hiring big, because the city was doing all the design for the freeways. This actually started before World War II. The engineering forces of the city were the first to design the freeways. After the war, the city did freeway design under contract to the state division of highways. What is now CALTRANS gradually developed its own design forces and eventually took this work away. I came in as a part of the young team of engineers being hired to work on freeway design. That's what caught my imagination, because I had grown up wanting to be an architect (but saw that wouldn't do) and then a civil engineer with a scientific basis to build and design things. So I stayed with L.A. for 35 years because the city was exploding with growth. Not that you couldn't escape, but you were caught up in the excitement of what it meant to a young engineer—the opportunities to build and create. The need was there. I had chances to go elsewhere, but I never saw a greater need than where I was."

Source: Ann Keating, "Reflections in Public Works—Donald Tillman," *APWA Reporter* (July 1989).

Of course, public works do not just influence the lives of engineers, laborers, or public officials. Public works also influence the ways in which all members of a community live. Therefore, it is always important to remember to consult sources of a wide variety of individuals within a community to see the ways in which a public works facility affected their lives. For instance, the introduction of water and sewer lines to a residence had a profound effect on the family(ies) living there. Some public works departments maintain records of when service connections were made to specific structures. Through these records, the introduction of improvements can be dated for individual homes, blocks, and neighborhoods. Other departments maintain billing information for one address, which provides interesting information regarding power, water, and sewer connections, as well as the cost of these improvements to individuals.

Homewood, Illinois The Village of Homewood, Illinois, is a suburb to the south of Chicago first settled at the turn of the century. Located along the Illinois Central Railroad, some early residents used daily trains to commute to jobs in downtown Chicago. The village government maintains a variety of records which might be useful to a public works historian working within the community. Sewer and water system maps, and utility bill records provide detailed information on the development of infrastructure systems within the community. When researching the connections involved with one single structure, the village building permit files are invaluable. The permit files are arranged by lot and include detailed records of the original builder, contractor, and owner of the property. The initial plans are part of these files, and they often include sought-after information about utility connections. Later permits provide information about improvements or additions, including further utility connections.

SUGGESTED READINGS

Much of the information that public works historians need is contained in more general local histories. They are an excellent place to begin. For help on locating and using local history sources, consult David E. Kyvig and Myron A. Marty, *Nearby History: Exploring the Past Around You* (Nashville: American Association for State and Local History, 1982). Other excellent sources for this information are the histories completed by Works Progress Administration (WPA) writers during the 1930s in many communities across the country as part of the

Federal Writers' Project. These histories provide a wealth of information about both the built environment and the residents within a community. Some of these WPA histories have been published in abridged form, but manuscript versions are often found in state or university archives. A guide to these histories is the American Historical Association's *Survey of Federal Writers' Project Manuscript Holdings in State Depositories.*

An excellent introduction to the use of oral history sources in local history is the chapter on oral documents in Kyvig and Marty. In addition, see: Willa K. Baum, *Oral History for the Local Historical Society*, 2nd edition, rev. (Nashville: American Association for State and Local History, 1977) and Barbara Allen and Lynwood Montell, *From Memory to History: Using Oral Sources in Local History Research* (Nashville: American Association for State and Local History, 1981).

A good introductory guide to public records is: H. G. Jones, *Local Government Records: An Introduction to Their Management, Preservation and Use* (Nashville: American Association for State and Local History, 1980). See also Maynard J. Brichford, *Archives and Manuscripts: Appraisal and Accessioning* (Chicago: Society of American Archivists, 1977). In addition, two groups can provide further assistance: National Information Center for Local Government Records, 172 Second Avenue, N., Suite 102, Nashville, TN 37201; and the Society of American Archivists, Chicago, IL. Gerald Danzer, *Public Places: Exploring Their History* (Nashville: American Association for State and Local History, 1987) provides a starting point for finding and using maps, plats, building plans, and other public resources.

PART II

MAKING THE INVISIBLE VISIBLE

Chapter 4

NETWORKS THAT
TIE HOMES TO A COMMUNITY

Public works connect individuals to communities and communities to each other. There are two distinct types of infrastructure networks that local historians can examine: those that physically tie individuals (through their homes and businesses) to community public works systems (such as sewer lines); and those that tie a community to a region and beyond (such as highways).

Historians have in recent decades begun the task of reconstructing the development of public works within specific communities, mainly through case studies of the earliest and largest systems. So the best-known history is that of large cities and the introduction of major infrastructure systems. What is not as well known, or not known at all, is the means by which smaller communities—towns and suburbs—adopted these services. A major task before local researchers is to uncover the public works history of small and middle-sized communities across the North America.

Public works provide unusual perspectives on a community's past. When community residents first developed a public water supply, laid sewer pipe, paved roads, or lit their streets with gas or electric power, all tell us a great deal about daily life in these communities. In addition, they point us to the most important community concerns of the day. Information about service systems in smaller localities also can be compared with the existing timelines for the development of infrastructure systems, based largely on research in large cities. This will provide a much stronger picture of infrastructure development by including a wide range of communities, not simply the largest places.

This chapter provides a picture of what is now known about the history of public works networks. It is most definitely a work-in-progress. Local historians, with an interest in public works, can improve this picture by setting their community's history alongside this general outline. Questions to consider as the stories unfold are: how does the history of a specific community confirm or counter this general picture?; and why do these similarities/differences exist?

INDUSTRIALIZATION
AND URBAN INFRASTRUCTURE

Homes and businesses are today tied together through a wide range of service networks: water, sewers, electricity, gas, telephone, and cable systems. Most of these systems are buried below the ground. It is hard to imagine, but true that even one hundred years ago few of these services ran into most homes and businesses across the country. Initially, only the residents in the largest cities had access to these infrastructure systems.

The change in the nineteenth century which led to the creation of service networks in urban areas was industrialization. Large-scale manufacturing set into motion changes in the scale of production and consumption that led to dramatic growth in cities across North America and Europe in the nineteenth century. For instance, the population of New York was just over 60,000 in 1800; by 1890 over 2,500,000 people resided there. Chicago grew from under 300 people in 1830 to over 1,000,000 in 1890.

Joel A. Tarr and Gabriel Dupuy in their recent book, *Technology and the Rise of the Networked City in Europe and America*, describe the connection between industrialism and the growth of service networks:

> Although technology and cities have always been interdependent, only since the advent of industrialism in the nineteenth century have urban technological networks evolved. Today, what we call the **urban infrastructure** provides the technological "sinews" of the modern metropolitan area: its road, bridge, and transit networks; its water and sewer lines and waste-disposal facilities; and its power and communication systems. (xiii)

Perhaps at no time was the contrast between urban and rural living so dramatic as in the second half of the nineteenth century. In the largest cities, running water, sewerage hookups, telephone lines, and gas and electric connections all transformed daily life. Urban homes became more intimately and physically attached to the communities around them largely through new underground utility networks. But in outlying towns and villages—not to mention the rural areas—life

In St. Louis, private streets served several wealthy developments in the late nine-teenth century. By privately providing streets, lighting, and parks, developers and residents maintained complete control of the process and bypassed the often cum-bersome improvement process. In recent decades, planned unit developments (PUDs) have taken a similar route to improvements. *Photograph by David Beito; courtesy of the Public Works Historical Society of the American Public Works As-sociation, Kansas City, Missouri.*

was much as it had been, because initially these systems were available only in the inner core of the nation's largest cities. One of the central questions which local historians, researching those smaller towns and villages, need to ask is whether industrialization was as crucial to the introduction of service networks in small communities as it was in the largest cities.

STREETS

While sewers, water pipe, and underground power conduits are in-visible networks, streets are a basic, and visible, public work. For cen-turies, streets served as the basic circulation system tying homes and businesses together. Streets not only provide avenues for the movement of urban residents, but also right-of-way for underground and access routes for above-ground service networks, such as police, fire, schools, and parks. Streets are the public "glue" that hold parcels of private property together as a community.

In this respect, the original plat of a subdivision within a community is an important organizing force for both visible and invisible infrastructure networks over the whole of a community's history. The subdivision plat identifies basic areas of public and private space, primarily by dividing the land into individual lots and streets. The width of streets varies over time and across the continent. Sometimes the streets are brand new creations, while at other times they reflect roads already in existence, but never officially dedicated to public use. While streets are generally controlled by local government, sometimes they remain under the private control of a community association.

St. Louis, Missouri During the late nineteenth century, several real estate developers in St. Louis subdivided outlying tracts of land around private streets and parks. These developers set up a property owners' association to maintain the common lands within the subdivision—the square at the center of the tract, and the surrounding streets. The initial homeowners built expensive homes, and the property owners' association cared for the common grounds. Unlike other residents of St. Louis, the residents on private streets came together to pay for repairs and improvements; they did not turn to local government.

David Beito, a historian who has studied these private places, found Vandeventer Place, developed in the 1870s, to be one of the most ambitious developments in St. Louis:

> At its height, Vandeventer Place contained within its boundaries the cream of St. Louis society. One mansion cost over $800,000 to build in the 1870s (about $8 million in 1989 dollars). The size of the subdivision complemented the scale of the houses. It comprised two complete city blocks of eighty-six residences thus dwarfing all previous private places. To guard against commercial encroachments, the developers erected a veritable Maginot Line of rear carriage houses. A park median, a feature borrowed from Benton Place [an earlier private place in St. Louis], ran the length of the street.

Source: David Beito, "Owning the 'Commanding Heights': Historical Perspectives on Private Streets," in "Public-Private Partnerships: Privatization in Historical Perspective," *Essays in Public Works History* 16 (1989): 5.

Today, while complaints about potholes abound, most streets in communities across the country are paved. This was not the case in most communities only a hundred years ago. Dirt roads were the rule, and rainy stretches turned streets into large mudholes. As cities industrialized, businesses needed better roads to move materials and finished products. As Larry McNally notes in *Building Canada: A History of Public Works*, "[b]y necessity, cities became experimenters in road surfacing. Toronto, for example, tried cedar blocks in the late 1860s, granolithic pavements (concrete) in 1886, asphalt in 1888, and brick paving blocks in 1893."

The history of pavements is a fascinating glimpse at changes beneath our feet. Over the course of the nineteenth and early twentieth century a variety of pavements were used, and all had problems. Wood blocks, although not slippery when wet, were not durable; stone was durable, but slippery when wet. By the early part of the twentieth century, asphalt and concrete emerged as the most enduring and useful pavements.

A little investigation in almost any community will yield some stretch of street or sidewalk with older pavement—cobblestone or brick—that gives physical evidence of older pavement choices. Looking back at city council notes or public works department records can provide an abundance of information about work done on a particular street. In many communities, business interests pushed for hard pavements in the commercial district, while residential streets remained unpaved for years.

PUBLIC TRANSPORTATION

Until after the Civil War, urban residents primarily used streets for walking or for riding on horses or in carriages. Streets were public works, the mode of transportation private. Historians describe these communities as "walking cities" or "pedestrian cities." Over the course of the nineteenth century, though, new transportation networks developed in the largest cities: omnibuses, commuter railroads, streetcars, cable cars, and elevated railroads. While most urbanites continued to walk to work through the turn of the last century, public transportation systems were increasingly available.

Between 1890 and 1917 streetcars enjoyed tremendous growth across the United States. Ridership on street railways jumped from 2 billion in 1890 to more than 5 billion in 1902 to 11 billion in 1917. Virtually all streetcar systems in the United States during these years were privately controlled. Some well-to-do residents rode commuter railroad lines to suburban enclaves. Many middle-class residents be-

Horsecars began to appear in North American cities in the 1830s and were quite common by the late 1850s in larger urban areas. A team of horses led a car—which was often open air—along a track laid in the street pavement on a regular route through urban areas. This photograph shows a Pittsburgh horsecar in the early 1860s. By the 1880s, cable cars and electric streetcars began to replace horsecars. *Courtesy of the Pennsylvania Room, Carnegie Library of Pittsburgh, Pittsburgh, Pennsylvania.*

gan to use streetcars and settled several miles from the central business district. The working class continued to live close to factories and other unskilled jobs, because they could not afford the cost of commuting. Over the course of several generations, cities and towns which had a mixture of people and uses began to develop far more specialized patterns.

Engineers played an important role in developing these new forms of urban transportation. Engineer Bion J. Arnold pioneered the modern electric railway and developed one of the first comprehensive studies of urban transportation for Chicago. Trained as a mechanical engineer at Hillside College in Michigan, Arnold set out to learn as much about engineering as he could. As historian Paul Barrett explains:

Beginning as a draftsman, he soon moved on to a Dubuque, Iowa, iron-works, for which he designed cable railway machinery and reciprocating steam engines. In 1887 he moved on to the Chicago Great Western Railroad, redesigning some of its locomotives during his short tenure there. It was at this point that the blossoming field of electrical engineering attracted Arnold's attention.

After post-graduate work at Cornell University, Arnold was hired as a consulting engineer by the Thompson-Houston Company—later part of General Electric. As consulting engineer for the company which was to transport visitors around the Chicago World's Fair of 1893, Arnold supervised the construction of the first successful third rail rapid transit system. . . . For the next twelve years, transit building and invention comprised a major part of Arnold's activities. He became, as one contemporary biographer observed, "a master of mathematical theory and electrical practice."

Among the projects that Arnold supervised were: the St. Charles Street Railway in New Orleans; an electric interurban between Chicago and Milwaukee; tunnels on the Grand Trunk, New Haven, and Erie railroads; and electrification of 300 miles of track around New York City.

In addition to meeting the technical challenges of urban transit at the turn of the century, Arnold turned to related urban policy questions. In 1902, the Chicago City Council commissioned Arnold to assess Chicago's mass transit system. Arnold produced a report which was the "first comprehensive engineering study of urban mass transit." Arnold believed that regulated private ownership could provide excellent service. He believed that "transit should be privately owned to retain the spur of the profit motive and to insulate it from politics."

Source: Paul Barrett, "People in Public Works—Bion Joseph Arnold," *APWA Reporter*, (September 1982): 5–6.

The shift from private to public ownership of mass transit systems began at the turn of the century as some transit companies encountered financial difficulties. In 1912, San Francisco was the first municipality to enter the electric street railway field. In 1919, Seattle took over a bankrupt system, followed by Detroit in 1922, New York in 1932, Cleveland in 1942, and Boston and Chicago in 1947. By 1975, publicly owned companies carried over 91 percent of the total ridership in the United States.

Why did mass transit move from private to public hands? Clearly, competition from jitneys, buses, and automobiles, beginning around

Interurbans were familiar sights in many communities across North America until the Second World War. Powered by overhead electric lines, interurban systems connected suburban and rural communities long before automobiles and buses oriented movement between communities along highways. The introduction of electric power into businesses and homes within many communities was also tied to the arrival of these electrically powered interurbans. Look for evidence of interurbans today along bike trails or current highway routes. *Courtesy of the Public Works Historical Society of the American Public Works Association, Kansas City, Missouri.*

World War I, led to losses in both riders and revenues for transit companies. As the ratio of people to automobiles moved downward from eleven in 1920 to two in 1970, private systems without public subsidies could no longer survive. Historians have begun the task of examining mass transit primarily as it unfolded in the major metropolitan areas. However, the suburban communities' view is often missing from this story, which emphasizes the central business district. Locating old streetcar and cable lines requires some detective work—as with old pavements—but a careful look around town may yield some physical evidence. Examine excavation sites in the commercial district of a community whenever street or infrastructure repairs are under way. Streetcar track is often uncovered in the course of maintenance work.

Another part of the story of mass transit, which is often overlooked as one moves out beyond the city center, is electric interurbans or streetcars. They ran beyond the limits of center cities and they were generally bigger and also faster than their urban cousins. In many regions of the country, they provided an important form of public transportation between communities that heretofore had no rail connections. Beginning in the closing years of the nineteenth century, interurbans grew in strength and numbers until the 1920s, when competition from automobiles and buses signaled their eventual decline. Many interurbans ran in areas that today are a part of metropolitan regions. They facilitated travel between small communities and into larger hubs in a pre-automobile era. Some lines ran far from major metropolitan areas, linking work, home, and leisure sites for rural and small-town residents. One turn of the century line ran from Bennington, Vermont, to Williamstown, Massachusetts. Another connected communities up and down the Fox River Valley from Elgin to Aurora, Illinois.

Los Angeles, California The once-distinctive suburban sprawl of the Los Angeles metropolitan region is generally attributed to the rise of the automobile. Interestingly, it is perhaps more the result of an extensive interurban system that linked industrial, commercial, and residential areas in southern California beginning in the 1890s. Henry E. Huntington built and organized interurban lines across the Los Angeles Basin between 1890 and 1910. At their peak, there were more than 1,000 miles of interurban track in the Los Angeles region. Huntington was as interested in selling land as he was interurban tickets. Thus, he used his interurbans to provide access to outlying subdivisions and began the process of suburban sprawl that we today associate with freeway development.

Source: Robert M. Fogelson, *The Fragmented Metropolis, Los Angeles, 1850–1930* (Berkeley: University of California Press, 1993).

WATER SUPPLY

Together with streets and mass transit, historians know the most about water supply in the largest cities of North America. What they know is that until early in the last century, urban Americans relied on private sources of water. Most households drew their water from wells, streams, lakes, rivers, or rainwater cisterns. Wealthy urbanites could buy spring water from private sellers who delivered to private homes.

But in cities, problems with this private and individualistic approach appeared even in the decade after the American Revolution. As communities grew, many households could no longer count on a ready source of clean water. Either they did not have access to a private well, or they were too distant from a stream, river, or lake. Another problem that became evident as science came to better understand the transmission of disease was the quality of water. Although bacteria was not discovered until the 1880s, many doctors and public health advocates connected unclean water with disease years before. Epidemics of cholera and yellow fever during the late eighteenth and early nineteenth centuries spurred local communities to improve and increase their water supplies. While these problems worried residents, the threat of fire more often led to solutions for water supply problems. Fire was a possibility that threatened everyone, but it most endangered the biggest property holders. As a result, the business elite often pressured hard for a water system that could help avert complete disaster in case of fire.

Acquiring an adequate water supply was important to many different urban constituents—business and industries, homeowners, fire insurance companies, and those concerned with public health. City boosters considered waterworks as crucial in the competition between municipalities for population, trade, and industry. Urban businessmen and residents demanded adequate water for civic purposes, such as street flushing and fire hydrants, to eliminate pollution and in anticipation of future needs.

Philadelphia, Pennsylvania Yellow fever killed 4,000 in Philadelphia in 1793. Recurrences of the epidemic took place in 1794, 1797, and in 1798 when 3,500 died. Community residents demanded an improved water supply, although there was not yet a scientific connection between polluted water and the transmission of disease. In 1798 the Philadelphia City Council agreed to plans by Benjamin Latrobe to pump water from the Schuylkill River to Centre Square, where it would be distributed under the streets through bored wooden logs.

Latrobe was born in England and trained under the leading British civil engineer, John Smeaton. He came to the United States in 1796 to make his fortune. Latrobe was soon aware of his significant role in American engineering, as is clear from the following excerpt from a letter he wrote to his brother in 1807:

You are perfectly right in the difference you imagine that there is between doing business here and in England in my profession. Had I, in England, executed what I have done here, I should now be able to sit down quietly and enjoy otium cum dignitate. But in England, the croud [sic] of those whose talents are superior to mine is so great, that I should perhaps never have elbowed through them. Here I am the only successful Architect and Engineer. I have had to break the ice for my successors, and what was more difficult, to destroy the prejudices which the villainous Quacks, in whose hands the public works have hitherto been, had raised against the profession.

Latrobe completed his direction of the Centre Square Works in 1801. Philadelphians therefore received water from a central souce decades before other urbanites. In 1822, a much improved system, using new reservoirs built on Fairmount (a rocky hill where the Philadelphia Art Museum now stands) opened for operation with iron mains replacing the old wooden ones.

Source: Michael C. Robinson, "People in Public Works—Benjamin Henry Latrobe," *APWA Reporter* (December 1980): 4–6.

Initially, most cities turned to private companies to solve their water supply problems. Many worked from the successful experience of London, the largest city in the world in 1800. At that time, eight private companies each served specific parts of metropolitan London. Boston's water was supplied by a private company between 1796 and 1848; in Baltimore a private company provided water between 1807 and 1854; and in New York private efforts supplied water between 1798 and 1842.

What residents in most large cities found was that private companies simply did not have the economic interest or the large capital requirements needed to construct massive water systems. In the United States the percentage of publicly owned waterworks grew from 6.3 in 1800 to 53.2 in 1896. This trend was even more pronounced in large cities. In 1860 there were fifty-seven public and seventy-nine private water systems in the United States. The sixteen largest cities had public waterworks. The larger cities were more likely to have publicly owned waterworks and the smaller cities to have privately owned ones. By 1896 only nine of the country's largest cities still had privately owned waterworks.

In Canada, there were only three water supply systems in 1850: St. John, New Brunswick; Montreal; and Toronto. As in the United States, many early attempts at water provision were private. For instance, in

Close-up it might be difficult to identify the function of these buildings, which comprise the Fairmount Waterworks in Philadelphia before 1874. Cloaked in neoclassical facades, these massive structures bear some resemblance to other public buildings. Only the water intake tunnels at the bottom of the buildings provide important hints about their functions. Within any community, there are apt to be buildings such as these, whose public works function is difficult to decipher. *Courtesy of the Commissioners of Fairmount Park, Philadelphia, Pennsylvania.*

1801 Montreal's first water company was formed. This private enterprise constructed a simple water system sending spring water atop Mount Royal downhill in wooden pipes. During the 1870s, municipalities constructed twenty-three systems and seventy-five additional systems were built in the 1880s. By 1900, two hundred and thirty-five waterworks served Canadian cities.

This photograph shows a wider view of the surroundings of the Fairmount Waterworks seen close up in the preceding photograph. In the distance behind the waterworks buildings are the reservoirs which held water until it was needed. Viewing public works from different perspectives often helps to identify the functions of structures which initially might seem quite mysterious. *Courtesy of the American Philosophical Society, Philadelphia, Pennsylvania.*

When examining the history of water supply in any community, local historians should try to answer several questions. What precipitated the development of a community water supply? Was the first community water supply public or private? If private, did the system eventually become public? Why? How did the system work? How did people use it and pay for it? Answers to these questions are critical in understanding notions of community responsibility at a given point in the past, and will provide important counterpoints to information about the largest cities.

Marshalltown, Iowa The largest cities, which are most studied, built water systems in response to overcrowding, rapid growth, and industrialization. Interestingly, most American cities—hundreds of them—that built waterworks in the second half of the nineteenth century were cities with populations between 5,000 and 10,000 people. Why did these communities choose to build systems that were not essential to their health and immediate well-being?

Historian Maureen Ogle has taken a look at three such communities

While most communities across North America have water systems, some continue to rely on human labor to bring water into homes. Here, boys in El Cerrito, New Mexico, serve as the water delivery system, using water drawn from a nearby stream. Local historians can explore the ways in which residents accessed a water supply before a community system was put in place, and consider the ways in which these earliest water sources affected settlement patterns. *Courtesy Bureau of Agricultural Economics, Washington, D.C.*

in Iowa: Boone, Marshalltown, and Iowa City. While the populations of these three towns remained under 10,000 before 1895, Ogle found that each built waterworks. She explains that "the decision to build waterworks involved more than a reflex response to urban growing pains. Rather, the introduction of this important municipal utility actually facilitated urban growth, without the stimulus of some external crisis." In addition, Ogle explains that residents demanded a municipal water supply "not only for firefighting but for domestic and manufacturing purposes as well." By the 1870s, residents in these three Iowa towns found that a water supply was an essential distinction between cities of "considerable size" and "smaller towns," that is, not the size but the outlook of the community as reflected in the decision to build a municipal water supply.

Source: Maureen Ogle, "Redefining 'Public' Water Supplies, 1870–1890: A Study of Three Iowa Cities," *The Annals of Iowa* 50 (Summer 1990): 507–530.

Another important question to consider is the source of water. Communities such as Lowell, Massachusetts, Patterson, New Jersey, and Toronto, Ontario, drew their water from sources close at hand. Other communities, such as San Francisco, New York, and Winnipeg, rely on distant water supplies. Water sources are largely determined by area resources. In some cases, however, developments outside the region are central. For example, the federal government's completion of the Hoover Dam allowed for the diversion of Colorado River water to Los Angeles hundreds of miles to the west.

San Francisco, California The growth of San Francisco in the late nineteenth century necessitated an expansion in its water supply system. Prior to the 1848 gold rush, San Francisco obtained its water from shallow wells and springs. Later, barges brought water across the bay from Marin County while another effort diverted water from a nearby stream into the city. All of these were private efforts, and only in 1900 did the San Francisco City Council attempt a public system. By 1901, the municipality made its first application to the federal government to divert water from the Tuolumne River which ran through Hetch Hetchy Valley in Yosemite National Park. Preservationists mounted a strong campaign against the Hetch Hetchy plan, and not until 1913 did San Francisco receive federal authorization for construction of the project. Michael Maurice O'Shaughnessy served as city engineer for the length of the project. Historian Jeffrey K. Stine describes the magnitude of the project:

[T]he Hetch Hetchy water and power supply system dwarfed other city public works projects. It was one of the major public works endeavors of its day. Taking 20 years to complete, it required construction of a 68-mile standard-gauge railroad, two large storage dams, four hydraulic power-plants, and a complex system of aqueducts, tunnels, and pipe lines which conveyed water by gravity flow 150 miles through two mountain ranges to San Francisco.

Source: Jeffrey K. Stine, "People in Public Work—M. M. O'Shaughnessy," *APWA Reporter*, (March 1979): 4–5.

SEWER SYSTEMS

One of the largest public works structures in many communities is a sewage pumping and treatment facility. Every community that has a sewerage system has one or more such structures. Sewage pumping stations often date back to the later part of the nineteenth century, while treatment plants were usually constructed during the middle of the twentieth century. These structures offer an important visible reminder of one of the most significant invisible networks in North American communities today.

Until the 1850s, household wastes were disposed of through private and small-scale means in most communities. Privy vaults and cesspools served most urban residences, which were periodically emptied by private scavengers. Urbanites constructed the first sewer systems for groundwater, not wastewater. In Boston, residents constructed the wooden conduits to drain their cellars in the seventeenth century. By the early 1700s, some of these drains were connected to form the earliest common sewers under Boston's streets. Local government regulated these initially private efforts. In New York, private initiative built storm sewers across lower Manhattan in the late eighteenth and early nineteenth centuries.

Both public and private sewers constructed before 1850 were designed not for wastewater, but for stormwater drainage. The increasing size of United States cities, and the development of large-scale waterworks fostered a wastewater disposal crisis by the 1850s. Population densities in the largest cities in North America increased substantially by the mid-nineteenth century, and overflowing privies and cesspools became a health hazard. A constant flow of water provided to households by new public water systems exacerbated sanitation problems, as wastewater flowed into existing cesspools, yards, and alleys.

Systematic sewer building was spurred by prevailing notions of contagious disease in the mid-nineteenth century. Disease did not distinguish rich from poor. The six cholera epidemics that swept North America between 1832 and 1873 showed the deadly strength of contagion. While mid-century physicians did not understand that underlying viruses or bacteria were responsible for these epidemics, they were convinced that disease was caused by bad air, called miasma. Miasma arose above filthy and polluted areas, and physicians believed that sewer systems would help to carry off the filthy wastes that were thought to cause disease.

Brooklyn, New York Engineers developed the critical expertise necessary for the development of sewerage systems in cities across North America. One of the earliest and most prominent among these engineers was Julius Walker Adams, who designed the Brooklyn sewer system.

Born in Boston in 1812, Adams had little formal engineering training. After two years at West Point, he went to work for various railroads in the Middle West. In 1846 Adams worked on the construction of the Cochituate waterworks in Boston. In 1857 the citizens of Brooklyn called on him to prepare a comprehensive plan for a system of sewers for the city. This was his first major project, and a challenging one. At this time no American city had been sewered following a general plan.

Brooklyn then covered an area of 20 square miles, much of which was then considered suburban territory. The call for a sewerage system in Brooklyn was not fueled by large-scale public health problems—as it was in nearby Manhattan—but by the desire to improve drainage in anticipation of substantial urban development. Adams later remembered:

> At that date we were totally without data of any kind in this country to guide in the determination of the proper dimensions of sewers for the drainage of cities and towns. No gaugings had ever been made of the discharge of sewers. and the only principle recognized was to make the sewers large enough to admit entrance of workmen to clean them by the use of the pick and shovel; so little had the subject occupied the attention of engineers that it was scarcely thought within their province, in this direction to do more than to see to the proper construction of what was determined upon by property owners, city surveyors, or municipal councils.

Adams remained undaunted by the task. He researched sewerage systems and theories then in favor in Europe and set about adapting them for use in Brooklyn. In the process he became an advocate of "simplicity and cheapness" in sewerage works. By this he did not mean "the use of second rate materials or workmanship, neither of which should find place in any works of sewerage," but "to the economy which results from the adoption of methods of design strictly suited in character, materials and workmanship in the simplest manner, to the end in view."

His approach was highly successful. Adams took as his guide the English "water-carriage" system. He laid no claim whatever to its originality, but only that he had adopted it for use in Brooklyn. He did point with pride in 1889 to a system so well designed that "an experience of over 20 years points to no modification being called for in the original design or scheme beyond matters of detail." Following the design of the Brooklyn sewerage system, Adams remained in the New York area as a public works director. In 1880 Adams wrote the first comprehensive text on the principles and practices of sewering towns and cities in the United States, *Sewers and Drains for Populous Districts*, based on his successful experience in Brooklyn.

Julius Walker Adams was part of an important generation of engineers who helped launch modern America. With little formal training, Adams became one of the leading sanitary engineers in the United States. He did so through practical experience and careful study of existing systems. Adams advised cities and towns across the country on the difficult choices they faced in providing adequate sewerage for the health and safety of their communities.

Source: Ann Keating, "People in Public Works—Julius Walker Adams," *APWA Reporter*, (November 1988): 26–27.

In some communities, the homeowners on a single street banded together to build a private sewer. But this was not a realistic solution to a problem whose solution had to be community-wide if it were to be effective. Municipalities like Brooklyn and Chicago constructed the first planned municipal sewer systems in the late 1850s. Residents in New York City and Washington, D.C., undertook construction of sewer systems in the years after the Civil War. However, extensive sewer construction did not begin until researchers settled basic design questions, including the separate versus combined sewer question, at the turn of the century.

In Canada, most cities constructed sewers before 1914. Doctors, civil engineers, and social reformers led the push for sewer systems, which often met fierce resistance from ratepayers during the economic

Julius Walker Adams was a prominent nineteenth-century engineer who worked on significant public works projects. Good sources for information about engineers involved in public works projects in a community are national engineering journals and newsletters. In particular, member obituaries ran regularly in these publications. The American Society of Civil Engineers published *A Biographical Dictionary of American Civil Engineers* (1972) which includes more than 170 biographies of prominent engineer born before 1860. *Courtesy of the Public Works Historical Society of the American Public Works Association, Kansas City, Missouri.*

downswing which followed Confederation in 1867. For instance, Toronto residents vetoed improved sewage facilities twice during the 1880s, rather than bear increased costs. Questions were also raised about whether sewers should be constructed for all residents or only for those who could afford them. In St. John, for instance, wealthy residents vetoed the extension of public sewers into the poorer districts.

Only the largest cities could afford to hire an engineering staff to design, build, and maintain sewer (or water) systems. Smaller cities hired skilled engineers from large urban areas as consultants to design their systems. As well, in the late nineteenth century, two national firms—the Holly and Worthington companies—sold pressurized water systems to middle-sized and small communities across North America. Communities as diverse as Iowa City, Iowa, and Shrevesport, Lousiana, considered installing these manufactured water systems.

In the 1930s, Public Works Administration (PWA) monies aided system construction in smaller cities and towns in the United States. The PWA was organized by the Roosevelt administration with the twin goals of improving infrastructure and fostering economic recovery. Even with federal aid, many rural and suburban communities have avoided the tremendous expense of sewerage systems through the use of private septic tanks.

Generally though, public agencies construct and maintain sewerage systems because of their high cost and the difficulty of charging customers more than a hookup fee. This contrasts with water systems, where annual water rents and fees provide a firm financial base. The relative ease of measuring water usage and the concurrent inability to easily measure sewerage use foster very different financial foundations.

Local historians investigating the introduction of a sewerage system may want to explore some of the following questions: was the original system designed for groundwater or wastewater (or both); did this distinction change over time; who was (were) the engineer(s) that designed the system; what was the specific impetus for the development of the system; how was it financed; and how far did the original system extend?

Of course, the story of sewerage goes beyond the confines of the sewer system. Untreated sewage continued to be a public health threat even after it was drained from under a community. This was particularly problematic when the same body of water was used as a water supply and a destination for raw sewage. State and local governments responded to these problems through regulation. For instance, by the late 1870s, the Massachusetts State Legislature was already passing laws that forbade the dumping of raw sewage into waters used for a domestic water supply.

It was well into the twentieth century before most communities embarked on the expensive task of constructing a sewage treatment works. By that time, engineers had developed successful treatment processes. During the Depression, the federal government provided

Sewage treatment plants are largely a twentieth-century innovation. In addition, municipalities have constructed water filtration plants primarily in the last two generations. Often in large structures, filtration plants are generally found adjacent to a water source. This photograph shows the interior of a filtration plant in Nashville, Tennessee, showing a view of these plants which the general public seldom, if ever, is allowed to see. *Courtesy of the Public Works Historical Society of the American Public Works Association, Kansas City, Missouri.*

funds to construct sewage treatment plants in communities across the country.

Fort Collins, Colorado Often decades separated the initial activity to create a systematic sewerage system within a community and any attempt to treat this sewage before it was discharged into the most readily available body of water. While residents in Fort Collins developed a sewerage system in the nineteenth century, it was not until 1932 that they began consideration of sewage treatment. Residents noted that neighboring communities of Greeley, Windsor, and Loveland had built sewage treatment plants with Works Progress Administration (WPA) funds. As Erin Christensen and Karen Waddell relate, "Uncle Sam's generosity did not interest folks in Fort Collins. They were leery of the WPA and federal involvement in local affairs. Their chief complaint was that in other projects the WPA failed to provide as much financial aid as expected. . . . Public Works Authority (PWA) grants for sewage plants were being awarded in Colorado. However, did Fort Collins really want federal money? The answer was yes and no." While residents would gladly take federal funds, they were less willing to raise taxes or float bond issues to pay the local portion of the bill.

The City of Fort Collins continued to debate the construction of a sewage treatment plant during the war years, but still could reach no consensus on devoting local funds to the project. By that point, the State of Colorado had been citing Fort Collins for health violations for years. In 1945, the federal government provided funds to design the sewage treatment plant, and in 1946 Fort Collins residents approved a bond issue of $250,000 to cover its cost. The facility finally opened in 1948.

Source: Erin Christensen and Karen Waddell, *How the Waste Was Won: A Century of Wastewater Services in Fort Collins, 1888–1988* (Fort Collins: City of Fort Collins, 1988).

SOLID WASTE DISPOSAL

Until now, discussion has centered on physical networks, whether visible—like streets—or invisible—like sewers and water lines. As well, now-invisible networks, such as streetcar systems, have been identified. Yet another kind of invisible public works network operating in most communities today is solid waste disposal. There are no wires or pipes that connect homes into this network, but it is a complex system nonetheless. Regular garbage pickup provides a temporal network that links homes within a community.

As with sewerage and water, solid waste disposal was essentially a private function well into the nineteenth century. Until then, households disposed of garbage by feeding it to animals, dumping it outside the city limits, or throwing it into yards and streets. As population—and concurrently population density—increased, municipalities contracted with private firms to haul off garbage from urban areas. By the 1890s, many municipalities began to organize their own solid waste departments to improve serve and guard the public health. Open trucks hauled garbage to city dump sites, and private scavengers collected recyclable materials such as paper, glass, iron, and rags. Closed trucks were introduced in the years after World War II. In the last several decades there has been a shift back from public provision of garbage disposal to contracting with private scavengers. Still, public agencies remain responsible for supervising this function.

Kalamazoo, Michigan At the turn of the century, women in communities across the country became involved in projects to clean up their streets and neighborhoods. Caroline Bartlett Crane was one of these women. As pastor of Kalamazoo's First Unitarian Church, Crane organized study groups to discuss urban problems, including water supply, police and fire protection, and sewage and waste disposal practices.

In 1904, Crane established the Women's Civic Improvement League. One of the league's first projects was to supervise street cleaning in central Kalamazoo for three months. Crane, using a system initiated by George E. Waring in New York City, set white-uniformed sweepers to work. Historian Suellen Hoy notes that:

> By the end of the project, the league had demonstrated that the Waring system was sanitary, efficient, and economical. Residents agreed that Main Street was cleaner than it had ever been. By quickly bagging the swept and piled dirt, it was not blown into nearby homes and businesses, and the sweepers did not waste time gathering and handling the same dirt again and again. No longer were two-horse wagons, with two men stopping to pick up bagged dirt and rubbish, used; one-horse carts, driven by one man, not only proved adequate but brought savings in time and labor.

Because of the success of this project, Crane was asked to conduct sanitary surveys in communities across the country. While few achieved the prominence of Crane, women across the country took a similar interest in the urban environment and worked to improve it. Crane provides one important reason for this interest in her 1907 essay "The Making of an Ideal City":

> We certainly should keep our city—that is to say, our common home—clean. The individual houses and premises, the schools, the places of public assembly, the places of trade, the factories, the places where foods are prepared, sold, served, should be clean. There should be sanitary collection and disposal of all wastes that inevitably accumulate wherever human beings have a home and find habitation.

Source: Suellen Hoy, "People in Public Works—Caroline Bartlett Crane," *APWA Reporter*, (June 1978), pp. 7–8.

Since garbage collection has been a municipal responsibility in many communities for over a century, the disposal sites for waste have grown and changed. Historians are involved in researching the location and contents of historical garbage dumps in an effort to uncover this history, as well as to protect public health. Garbage dumps of more recent vintage may have been in sanitary landfills. When filled, these areas have been converted to parkland or other innovative uses.

Historians are also involved in a related task—tracking down the disposal of hazardous wastes from the past. Many industries, including iron, steel, tanning, and chemicals, have left a hazardous residual in and around their sites for decades. Local historians are in a particularly good position to aid in this detective work, using maps, city directories, and tax records to identify where hazardous wastes are likely to be located. The role of protector of public health is one that local historians may find unusual. However, their knowledge of past industrial and commercial uses of land within their communities is vital to the process of identifying potential hazardous waste sites. Historians may find challenging careers in this area in the years to come.

Lake Calumet, Illinois Craig E. Colten, a geographer working for the Illinois State Museum has done considerable research in the area of historical industrial wastes. One recent project led him to the Calumet region, on Chicago's southeast side, to explore the geography of industrial wastes.

Municipal garbage collectors have worked with a variety of equipment, at first using horsedrawn carts, then motor-powered enclosed trucks, and finally in recent decades, equipment which automatically loads garbage from cans or bins. Equipment has changed the demands on workers over time. In some communities garbage collectors even have been required to wear uniforms. *Courtesy of the Public Works Historical Society of the American Public Works Association, Kansas City, Missouri.*

Colten found that the Lake Calumet area provided an excellent setting for such research. Since 1869 it has been the scene of heavy manufacturing activity and because of the marshy conditions there, it has also been the site of extensive industrial waste disposal. Colten explains that:

> The use of historical methods can greatly aid researchers monitoring current environmental conditions. Through an analysis of historical documents, changing patterns of land use can be mapped, the location of disposal sites determined, and the composition of waste streams ascertained. This knowledge is particularly useful to hydrologists and geochemists attempting to locate plumes of contaminated groundwater. Application of historical methods to the Calumet situation helped develop a chronology of waste disposal techniques, and it will facilitate evaluation of other industrial areas in Illinois. The value of the chronology is that it aids in identifying the types of wastes that were commonly produced during certain periods and alerts researchers to how they were likely to have been discarded. Furthermore, examination of the historical record allows verification of what transpired in the past and decreases our dependence on speculation. Ultimately, this will prove useful in policy decisions regarding mitigation of hazardous waste disposal sites.

Source: Craig E. Colten, *Guidelines and Methods for Conducting Property Transfer Site Histories* (Champaign, IL: Hazardous Waste Research, 1987).

POWER SYSTEMS

Like streets, streetlights are a visible part of our infrastructure networks. Today, virtually all communities in North America have electric streetlights, which makes night travel both safer and easier. This was certainly not the case in eighteenth-century communities. In both the largest cities and the smallest villages, darkness after sundown was the rule.

Spurred by the example of London, where streets were lit by oil lamps, some of the largest communities in the United States began to provide street lamps by the end of the eighteenth century. A major improvement came in the early nineteenth century: illuminating gas. Baltimore, Maryland, was the first city in the United States (and only the third city in the world) to have a gas lighting system. In 1816, Rembrandt Peale, portrait painter and amateur scientist, organized the Gas Light Company of Baltimore which was chartered by the city council to lay gas pipes under city streets and provide street lamps. Other cities followed Baltimore's lead: New York in 1823, Boston in

At the turn of the twentieth century, electric streetlights dotted one of the bridges between Cambridge and Boston, Massachusetts. In many communities, movement to beautify city landscapes in the late nineteenth and early twentieth centuries lead to installation of elaborate ironwork streetlights, which served ornamental as well as functional purposes. If a community has subsequently adopted more utilitarian lights, it is sometimes possible to track down old fixtures in municipal warehouses. *Courtesy of the Public Works Historical Society of the American Public Works Association, Kansas City, Missouri.*

1828, New Orleans and Louisville in 1832, Philadelphia in 1836, and Washington D.C. in 1847. Similarly, in Canada private companies provided gas street lamps in Montreal after 1837 and in Quebec City after 1848. By 1850, there were over 300 gas light companies in the United States.

The specific means of providing service varied from community to community during the mid-nineteenth century. In some, the municipality owned the gas company outright, while in others service contracts were made with private gas companies. While gaslight illuminated larger communities, whale oil lamps sufficed in most communities until 1858, when coal oil or kerosene were also used in street lamps.

One interesting note about the history of gas provision is that until the introduction of electricity to compete with gas as a means of illumination, gas was used exclusively for lighting. When it became clear that electricity was far brighter and cleaner, gas companies began to market alternative uses for gas power: first for cooking and hot water heating, then for space heating and as an energy source for industry. This is an excellent example of avoiding obsolescence by creative reuse, for the gas industry had by the beginning of the twentieth century extended its pipelines into millions of homes and industries. Conversion to these alternative uses allowed for the continued use (and profit potential) of this infrastructure system.

Electricity for street lighting proceeded rapidly after Thomas A. Edison's development of the incandescent lamp in 1878. San Francisco was the first community to adopt the new technology for streetlights in 1880; New York lit Broadway with electric lights in the same year. By 1882, New York had its first central generating station (steam-powered) and 5,500 street lamps in operation. By 1892 there were 235 municipally owned electric systems in the United States, and electricity was just beginning to be introduced into homes.

Canada also saw electrical developments during these years. Robert Burns McMiking installed the first electric lights in Victoria in 1883. The St. John Electric Light Company began providing service in 1884. Private efforts to change streetlights in Montreal from gas to electric met strong resistance from local gas companies.

In 1888, Fred H. Whipple who was the secretary for a Detroit special commission on street lighting alternatives made a national survey of then-current practices. He surveyed 147 cities and found a wide variation in the extent of service and its costs, as well as both contract and rental systems for street lighting. Michael C. Robinson and Suellen Hoy reprinted part of his report in their 1976 *History of Public Works in the United States*:

> Washington D.C. 87 public lamps—burn all night every night—cost 65 cents per night each. Lamp on poles, wires underground—yearly contract.

Wichita, Kansas. 75 lights—located at street intersections—burn until midnight—cost $100 per year each. Also use 120 gas lamps and 300 gasoline lamps.

Chattanooga, Tennessee. 30 lights burning all night—cost 33 cents per night—2 year contract.

Ogden, Utah. 18 lights at street intersections. 673 fee apart in the business section—cost $133 per year each.

Sacramento, California. 36 intersection lights, burn all night except on moonlight nights—cost $252 per light per year—2-year contract—overhead wires—city also has 193 gas lights.

Electricity was also widely used for streetcars by the turn of the century. With the existence of two large users—street lighting and public transportation—electric companies extended service in the larger communities in the country. Once the infrastructure system was in place, marketing to residential customers began. Initially electricity was sold solely for lighting in homes and businesses, but over time electrical appliances were introduced which increased the demand for residential service.

A look at one suburban community illustrates these trends. In 1885, the Village of Lombard, about 30 miles due west of Chicago along a railroad line, purchased six gasoline street lamps. At the turn of the century, streets were still lighted with gasoline lamps. In the first years of the twentieth century, Lombard emerged as a stop along the Chicago, Aurora and Elgin Electric Interurban Line. This interurban line not only provided public transit to neighboring communities, it also gave the community its first electric connections. The interurban company also ran a power enterprise, DuPage County Electric and Power Company, which sold power to local communities. In 1906 the Village of Lombard contracted with this company to provide fifty-two electric street lamps. The electric company installed arc lamps which were hung from telephone poles. In 1907 the year after the introduction of electric streetlights, the electric company began to solicit residential customers.

TELEPHONE AND CABLE ACCESS

Until the middle of the nineteenth century, homes and businesses had no direct communication ties with the larger community—certainly no phones or cable connections, but also no regular home delivery of mail. Householders had to leave their dwellings to talk face to face with friends or business associates. The telegraph and telephone transformed this traditional landscape by connecting homes and businesses through technological innovations.

The stories of Samuel Morse and Alexander Graham Bell are familiar ones in American history. Their inventions transformed our homes, our businesses, and our communities. Today, the telegraph connects far-flung communities in an instant—and is perhaps on the road to extinction. What is hard to imagine, but central to the job of local historians is to explore the earlier role of the telegraph as the first communications infrastructure which linked households and businesses within a single community.

Between the beginnings of telegraph communication systems in 1845 and the widespread introduction of the telephone by the mid-twentieth century, urban residents used the telegraph to communicate within their communities, as well as beyond them. Police departments used telegraph systems to instantaneously link their district offices, and early burglar-alarm systems in many cities depended upon it. Messenger services and other enterprises relied heavily on the telegraph to conduct business.

Private companies developed the infrastructure needed for the telegraph. Pole lines were run along railroad rights-of-way between cities and towns across the United States in the decades before and after the Civil War. Information, which had taken days and weeks to move from one part of the country to another, was now received within minutes. Open-wire pole lines soon became familiar sights in cities and towns, only to be forced underground by residents distressed by their unsightliness or frightened by their presence. By the turn of the century, telegraph lines were buried under city streets alongside water and gas lines.

This invisible network is now not only buried, but largely forgotten. After 1880, the telephone began to replace the telegraph as the primary means of telecommunication. The telephone took the telegraph one step further—from the transmission of the words alone to the voice and the words of individuals connected by a wire. Alexander Graham Bell and Elisha Gray both independently developed the telephone in the mid-1870s, but Bell received broad patent rights, and the Bell Company dominated the field for decades after.

Like the telegraph, the telephone required a physical infrastructure. By 1930, wires and switches criss-crossed North America. New Haven, Connecticut, was the site of the first commercial telephone switchboard in 1878. At that time, 21 households and/or businesses owned telephones and were linked by a central switchboard. Two years later,

By 1930 virtually all urban communities in the United States used electricity to power a wide array of appliances and lighting fixtures, but 90 percent of rural residents did not have access to electric connections. The Congress passed the Rural Electrification Act in 1936 as a part of New Deal measures to boost the American economy. By 1976, 98 percent of rural households in the United States had electric connections. Images such as this one showing utility poles outside Irwin, Iowa, became a familiar part of the American landscape. *Courtesy of the Bureau of Agricultural Economics, Washington, D.C.*

there were 138 exchanges in operation in the United States, with 30,000 subscribers. By 1887, there were over 150,000 subscribers and over 1,000 exchanges in the United States. Canada saw a similar explosion. By 1887 there were over 12,000 subscribers to telephone exchanges in the provinces.

Local historians have the opportunity to explore this early telephone history, to see the ways in which daily life changed by responding to questions such as: How expensive was it to purchase a telephone and subscribe to an exchange? Who owned a telephone? Who used it? Where was the telephone located in homes? What kind of disruption did laying telephone lines create within homes and between structures? How did the telephone affect the lives of men, women, and children?

The latest infrastructure network which North Americans have demanded for their residences is cable television. Over the last twenty years, cable television systems have begun operating in most major American cities. Coaxial cable distributes not water or power, but television programming. As with water or sewer systems, head-to-head competition between firms would involve a wasteful duplication of capital investment. Instead, most local communities have granted exclusive franchises to cable companies to provide monopolistic service to an area.

The current debates over franchise agreements and the process of installing this service provide us with a flavor of the historical debates which surrounded the installation of earlier services. Questions such as where the system would go, when it would be introduced, and how it would be financed are similar to those raised with earlier services. Local historians can see some of the problems related to introducing new infrastructures into existing housing stock. Cable lines are often obtrusive and unsightly—running on top of outside walls and along interior ones.

Local historians can move here beyond history to policy questions. Local researchers, knowledgable in infrastructure history, can also help communities deal with new technologies and policy questions. Their research in infrastructure history can inform current political discussions whether concerning the best method of introducing a new sytem, uncovering potential hazards of past systems, or chronicling past debates on infrastructure. Good history is useful.

SUGGESTED READINGS

Historians have gone the furthest in exploring infrastructure systems in our largest cities. One of the clearest overviews of this work is Joel A. Tarr and Josef W. Konvitz, "Patterns in the Development of the Urban Infrastructure," in *American Urbanism: A Historiographical Review*, Howard Gillette, Jr., and Zane L. Miller, eds. (New York: Greenwood Press, 1987). For a useful discussion and bibliography see

Eugene P. Moehring, "Public Works and Urban History: Recent Trends and New Directions," *Essays in Public Works History*, 13 (1982). Another perspective is provided by Josef W. Konvitz in *The Urban Millennium: The City-Building Process from the Early Middle Ages to the Present* (Carbondale: Southern Illinois University Press, 1985).

The material on private streets in St. Louis is taken from David Beito, "The Private Places in St. Louis," in "Privatization: Public-Private Partnerships in Historical Perspective," *Essays in Public Works History*, 16 (1990). On changing street pavements, see Clay McShane, "Transforming the Use of Urban Space: A Look at the Revolution in Street Pavements, 1880-1924," *Journal of Urban History*, 5 (May 1979): 279-307.

On the interurbans in the Los Angeles area see: Spencer Crump, *Ride the Big Red Car: How Trolleys Helped Build Southern California* (Los Angeles, 1965). For an overview of the history of urban mass transportation see: Glen Holt, "The Main Line and Side Tracks: Urban Transportation History," *Journal of Urban History*, 5 (February 1979): 397-405; Mark S. Foster, "Delivering the Masses: Recent Excursions in Transportation History," *Journal of Urban History*, 7 (May 1981): 381-90; Charles Cheape, *Moving the Masses: Urban Public Transit in New York, Boston, and Philadelphia, 1880-1912* (Cambridge: Harvard University Press, 1980); Clay McShane, *Technology and Reform: Street Railways and the Growth of Milwaukee, 1887-1900* (Madison: Wisconsin State Historical Society, 1974); and George R. Taylor, "The Beginnings of Mass Transportation in Urban America, Part I," *Smithsonian Magazine of History* (1966): 31-54.

Four studies that consider the effects of mass transportation on growth in Chicago, Los Angeles, Boston, and Pittsburgh respectively: Paul Barrett, *The Automobile and Urban Transit: The Formation of Public Policy in Chicago, 1900-1930* (Philadelphia: Temple University Press, 1983); Scott Bottles, *Los Angeles and the Automobile: The Making of the Modern City* (Berkeley: University of California Press, 1987); Sam Bass Warner, *Streetcar Suburbs: The Process of Growth in Boston, 1870-1900* (Cambridge: Harvard University Press, 1962); and Joel Tarr, "Transportation Innovation and Changing Spatial Patterns in Pittsburgh, 1850-1934," *Essays in Public Works History*, 6 (1978).

On water history in the United States, see Nelson P. Blake, *Water for the Cities: A History of the Urban Water Supply Problem in the United States* (New York: 1956); and Stuart Galishoff, "Triumphs and Failures: The American Response to the Urban Water Supply Problem, 1860-1923," in Martin V. Melosi, ed. *Pollution and Reform in American Cities, 1870-1930* (Austin: University of Texas Press, 1980).

The material on Iowa cities by Maureen Ogle is from "Redefining

'Public' Water Supplies, 1870–1890: A Study of Three Iowa Cities" *Annals of Iowa* 50 (Summer 1990): 507–530. Other studies of the development of municipal water supplies in specific communities include: James C. O'Connell, "Chicago's Quest for Pure Water," *Essays in Public Works History*, 2 (1976); Thomas F. Armstrong, "Not for 'Barter and Speculation': A Comparative Study of Antebellum Water Supply," [Fredricksburg, Lynchburg, and Staunton, Virginia] *Southern Studies*, 18 (Fall 1979): 304–319; John Ellis and Stuart Galishoff, "Atlanta's Water Supply: 1865–1918," *Maryland Historian*, 8 (Spring 1977):5–22; and Terry S. Reynolds, "Cisterns and Fires: Shreveport, Louisiana as a Case Study of the Emergence of Public Water Supply Systems in the South," *Louisiana History*, 22 (Fall 1981): 337–67.

The material on the development of a sewage treatment plant in Fort Collins, Colorado was drawn from Erin Christensen and Karen Waddell, *How the Waste Was Won: A Century of Wastewater Service in Fort Collins* (1988). For more information on the construction of sewage systems see Stanley K. Schultz and Clay McShane, "To Engineer the Metropolis: Sewers, Sanitation, and City Planning in Late-Nineteenth Century America," *Journal of American History*, 65 (September 1978): 389–411; Joel A. Tarr, "The Separate and Combined Sewer Problem: A Case Study in Urban Technology Design Choice," *Journal of Urban History*, 5 (May 1979): 308–339; Armstrong, Robinson and Hoy, *History of Public Works*, pp. 399–430; and Jon A. Peterson, "The Impact of Sanitary Reform Upon American Urban Planning, 1840–1890," *Journal of Social History* 13 (Fall 1979): 83–104. See also Louis P. Cain, "The Search for an Optimum Sanitation Jurisdiction: The Metropolitan Sanitary District of Greater Chicago, A Case Study," *Essays in Public Works History*, 10 (1981) and Carol Hoffecker, "Water and Sewage Works in Wilmington, Delaware, 1810–1910," *Essays in Public Works History*, 12 (1982).

On solid waste see Martin V. Melosi, "Pragmatic Environmentalist: Sanitary Engineer George E. Waring, Jr.," *Essays in Public Works History*, 4 (1977) and Melosi, *Garbage in the Cities: Refuse, Reform and Environment, 1880–1980* (College Station, TX: Texas A & M University Press, 1981). On recycling see Suellen Hoy and Michael C. Robinson, *A Handbook of Community Recycling Programs, 1890–1945* (Chicago: Public Works Historical Society, 1977).

The material quoted from Craig Colten is exerpted from a report entitled *Guidelines and Methods for Conducting Property Transfer Site Histories*, published by the Hazardous Waste Research and Information Center of the Illinois Department of Energy and Natural Resources (P.O. Box 5050, Station A, Champaign, IL 61820).

On electricity, see Thomas P. Hughes, *Networks of Power: Electrifica-*

tion in Western Society (Baltimore: Johns Hopkins University Press, 1983) and Harold Passer, *The Electrical Manufacturers* (Cambridge: Harvard University Press, 1953). Comparing three communities is Mark H. Rose and John G. Clark, "Light, Heat, and Power: Energy Choices in Kansas City, Wichita, and Denver, 1900–1935," *Journal of Urban History*, 5 (February 1979): 340–64. Harold Platt provides a specific case study of the development of electricity in Chicago. See *The Electric City* (Chicago: University of Chicago Press, 1991). See also, Ithiel de Sola Pool, ed., *The Social Impact of the Telephone* (Cambridge: MIT Press, 1977) for a series of edited essays on the social history of the telephone.

On cable television see Charles Jacobson, Steven Klepper, and Joel A. Tarr, "Water, Electricity, and Cable Television: A Study of Contrasting Historical Patterns of Ownership and Regulation," *Urban Resources*, 3 (Fall 1985): 9–18, 64; and Charles Jacobson, "Same Games, Different Players: Problems in Urban Public Utility Regulation, 1850–1987," *Urban Studies* 26 (1989): 13–31.

Chapter 5

NETWORKS THAT TIE A COMMUNITY TO A REGION

Networks not only tie homes to each other, but also tie communities to regions. Local historians can use public works as a vehicle to exploring the way in which a community is related to a region or a nation, as well as how local households are interrelated. The last chapter examined the connections between households, while this chapter will explore the links between communities' households.

One of the most important things to keep in mind throughout this discussion is that there is so much yet to be uncovered in public works history, particularly in relation to small and medium-sized communities across the country. So much of this story is yet to be written, and local historians are in advantageous positions to do so, with their keen understanding of community development.

TRANSPORTATION NETWORKS

Transportation networks tie local areas together as a region, and to the world beyond. An excellent place to begin to explore the local context of transportation history is to answer the following questions: How did the first settlers get to this community? Why did they stop here? How did the methods of moving in and out of the community change over time? By answering these three questions, local historians can create a basic outline that explains the ways in which a community fits into wider transportation networks at any point in time.

Reaching back to the colonial period, the British, Dutch, and French settled on or near the Atlantic Ocean, or alongside rivers or lakes. Water transportation provided the crucial links between small North

American communities and Europe. During this era, most settlement took place in a fifty-mile-wide band along the Atlantic Coast and inland along the St. Lawrence River. The largest cities, like New York and Baltimore, grew because of their fine natural harbors which facilitated trade. In the western United States, Spanish colonial public works like presidios reflect the hinterland status which these settlements maintained in Spanish America. In communities dating back to the colonial period, local historians may well find wharf or harbor improvements to be one of the earliest public works.

Before long, colonists along the Atlantic coast were eyeing land further inland. Before the American Revolution, George Washington had surveyed lands west of the Appalachians for his brothers' land company. Competing claims by the French for this same land helped to ignite the French and Indian War in 1754. After the Revolutionary War, Washington organized the Potomac Company and returned to the West. He advocated inland transportation improvements—canals and roads that would open western lands to British-American settlement—and raised public and private funds through the Potomac Company to build a turnpike road to Ohio and a canal to improve navigation on the Potomac River.

Washington also understood the need for trained engineers, not only to design fortifications to protect western lands, but to develop canals and roads. With few trained engineers in British North America, Washington and others lobbied for the establishment of the United States Military Academy at West Point. By the 1820s, engineers trained at West Point were involved in explorations and surveys, as well as in various federal construction projects related to internal improvements. The U.S. Army Corps of Engineers constructed a wide range of projects over the course of the nineteenth and twentieth centuries, including many related to flood control or military building.

While the Corps of Engineers aided in the development of early transportation networks, private enterprise fueled most improvements. During the first decades of the nineteenth century, private turnpike companies, chartered by state governments, were immensely popular. By 1850, there were hundreds of companies operating thousands of miles of roads. Private turnpikes provided much of the primary road network across the United States. Many communities in the eastern half of the nation bought stock in these turnpike companies in order to improve their relative position in the regional/national transportation hierarchy. It is worth a careful check in existing histories to see if there is any evidence for the involvement of your community in

The first federal works project stands at the mouth of Chesapeake Bay: the Cape Henry Lighthouse. Congress authorized construction of the lighthouse on August 7, 1789. President George Washington personally reviewed the bids, and the lighthouse went into service in October 1792. The Cape Henry Lighthouse helped guide ships through this hazardous area from October 1792 until it was retired from service in 1881. In 1881, the original lighthouse was replaced by a "new" black-and-white structure, but the Cape Henry lighthouse remains a popular tourist attraction. Both structures still stand, as seen in this photograph. Today it is owned by the Association for the Preservation of Virginia Antiquities. *Courtesy of the U.S. Coast Guard, Portsmouth, Virginia.*

such an enterprise. Evidence might include town council debates on stock subscriptions or construction reports in local newspapers.

Water networks provided the basic means of transportation in Canada for much of its history. Roads served as links between water networks and between communities. Many early roads were built along waterways—such as the road from Quebec to Toronto, which followed the St. Lawrence River and the Great Lakes.

Roads in the eighteenth and nineteenth centuries were constructed with materials readily available in the area. In much of Canada, residents took advantage of an abundance of trees to create corduroy roads. Corduroy roads were "paved" by laying tree trunks across the width of a road. Understandably, these roads did not provide much comfort to travelers traversing them. One Canadian woman, Anna Jamieson, described her experience:

> The road was scarcely passable; there were no longer cheerful farms and clearings, but the dark pine forest and the rank swamp, crossed by those terrific corduroy paths (my bones ache at the mere recollection) and deep holes and pools of rotted vegetable matter with water, black, bottomless, sloughs of despond.

Source: Larry McNally, "Roads, Streets and Highways," in *Building Canada: A History of Public Works*, Norman Ball, ed. (Toronto: University of Toronto Press, 1988): 31.

In DuPage County, Illinois, private companies developed several plank roads as turnpikes between 1847 and 1851. The plank road consisted of three-inch boards laid across stringers in the ground. Toll gates were set up approximately every five miles. One of these roads, the Southwestern Plank Road, was constructed at least in part using the funds provided by residents in communities such as Hinsdale and Naperville, which were in the projected path of the plank road.

While plank—or corduroy—roads or 150-year-old toll booths are unlikely to remain in any community today, there is one kind of physical evidence which remains. Roads that run at odd angles to the general subdivision pattern of a community often trace their roots to early highways and turnpikes (which were themselves often simply tracing earlier Indian pathways). Road names also provide a tipoff to early regional highways. For instance, on Chicago's northwest side, Milwau-

While corduroy or plank roads are no longer used in highway construction across North America, evidence of their past use remains. In this view of rural Canada in 1900, a rural road is being prepared for paving. A close look at the area under the road bed shows the rough edges of tree trunks which served as earlier road surfaces. Local historians might find similar layering on old roads within their communities. *Courtesy of the Public Works Historical Society of the American Public Works Association, Kansas City, Missouri.*

kee Avenue began as a highway running north to the settlement at Milwaukee.

Canals are also important parts of the transportation story in the first half of the nineteenth century. Between 1815 and 1860, approximately $195 million was expended by federal, state, and local governments—as well as private promoters—on U.S. canals. Virtually all of this activity took place east of the Mississippi River. The most extensive systems were found in New York, Pennsylvania, and Ohio. The most spectacularly successful was the Erie Canal, a 364-mile project between Albany and Buffalo, which linked the Atlantic Ocean with the Great Lakes. The most spectacularly unsuccessful canal effort was probably Indiana's attempt to connect Lake Erie with the Ohio River in a 450-mile canal.

From at least the middle of the 1700s, a canal between Albany and Buffalo, New York, had been discussed as a quicker and less expensive way of transporting goods and people between the Atlantic Coast and the Great Lakes. In 1817, after decades of false starts, the New York State Legislature authorized the construction of the 364-mile canal.

Few individuals in the United States had experience in canal building. The Erie Canal Board turned to the man who had surveyed the route of the proposed canal back in 1811—Benjamin Wright. His task was a difficult one:

> From the beginning of construction until the waters of Lake Erie flowed into the Atlantic Ocean eight years later in 1825, Wright confronted numerous obstacles. He sent his assistant, Canvass White, to England to study the British canals. White compiled vast amounts of information on the design and methods of canal construction. It took several false starts, however, to apply and modify the European practices of canal building to American materials and environment.
>
> Relying on persistence and ingenuity, Wright and his men constructed dams, locks, weirs, aqueducts, and reservoirs. They learned how to seal channels through puddling, to erect retaining walls, to make gravel beds impervious to water, and to fight malaria and other diseases. Limestone was discovered near the canal route, which answered the need for cheap, local hydraulic cement. New machines were developed that reduced strenuous hard labor, especially in removing matted earth and rocks, cutting roots and pulling stumps.
>
> Through the gradual process of trial and error, the men Wright hired eventually became highly competent canal builders. The Erie Canal thus became a virtual school of engineering, training a body of engineers that provided the expertise necessary to construct the new wave of internal improvements that was to sweep across the United States. Some of Wright's assistants, such as John B. Jervis, Canvass White, and Nathan Roberts, went on to occupy leading positions in the engineering profession.

Source: Rebecca Stine, "People in Public Works—Benjamin Wright," *APWA Reporter* (August 1982): 8–9.

The remains of a far-ranging canal system can be found across the eastern half of the United States. Tow paths, canals, and locks often remain as evidence of these transportation systems. This wooden lock along the Erie Canal is much like those originally constructed. *Courtesy of the Public Works Historical Society of the American Public Works Association, Kansas City, Missouri.*

Whether deemed an overall success or failure, canals, like turnpikes, strongly influenced communities along their way. Local historians investigating the history of nearby canals will encounter varying levels of physical evidence. In some cases, canals have been carefully restored and are maintained as historic sites. Congress has established a National Recreation Area in northeastern Ohio, along the route of a canal which once linked Lake Erie to the Ohio River. In other areas, canals are still a vital part of regional transportation networks. The St. Lawrence Seaway, opened in 1959, remains a vital shipping link between the Great Lakes and the Atlantic Ocean. In other cases, canals

WESTERN END OF THE GREAT ERIE CANAL.

As well as physical evidence of canals, old photographs or drawings aid local historians in their understanding of the workings of these systems. In this line drawing of the western end of the Erie Canal at Buffalo, New York, the way in which mules or horses pulled boats along the canal is illustrated. *Courtesy of the Public Works Historical Society of the American Public Works Association, Kansas City, Missouri.*

have been filled in and are difficult to find. Again, a look at standard local histories should provide initial information about the possible existence of a canal. Then the historian's task of filling in the pieces begins.

Lockport, Illinois One canal which has received official historic recognition is the Illinois and Michigan Canal. In 1984, federal action created the Illinois and Michigan Canal National Heritage Corridor and Commission. The commission has the mandate of working for the recreational, historic, and commercial-industrial development of the 120-mile-long urban cultural park. The original commissioners of the Illinois and Michigan Canal, which ran from Chicago to LaSalle by the late 1840s, were responsible for the platting of several towns along the way. Land grants to the canal company supported canal construction, so the commissioners encouraged the sale of lots. Chicago, LaSalle, Ottawa, Joliet, Utica, Marseilles, and Lockport were all laid out by the canal commissioners during the 1830s and owe their initial existence to the speculation surrounding this massive public work.

The chief engineer on this project, William Gooding, was convinced that water power was an important byproduct of the canal construction. Gooding designed water power stations along the canal route "to maximize the slight fall between the eastern terminus at Chicago and the western terminus 96 miles away." This emphasis on water power led to the establishment of the city of Lockport. As historian John Lamb explains: "At that city the largest fall on the course of the canal occurs. There is a drop of 40 feet in five miles between Lockport and neighboring Joliet. . . . The water power was used until the early twentieth century. Although use of the canal for hydraulic power increased, it never achieved what Gooding had hoped."

Source: John Lamb, "People in Public Works—William Gooding," *APWA Reporter* (December 1985): 4–5.

By the 1830s, communities across North America were linked by a transportation network consisting primarily of natural waterways, turnpikes, and canals. Settlements emerged and developed in concert with this evolving transportation network. The rules of the game changed dramatically during the 1830s, however, with the introduction of the railroad.

In hindsight, we know that railroads far outdistanced canals and turnpikes in most regional transportation systems, but from the 1830s to the 1850s, this point was not so clear. Thus, some communities continued to fund canals and turnpike systems rather than the railroad. Outside Chicago, the Village of Naperville turned down a railroad connection in the 1840s, because it envisioned continued prosperity from its turnpike. Naperville residents realized the error of this thinking as business and industry chose the nearby railroad town of Wheaton over their own community. Soon Naperville citizens sought their own railroad connections.

The railroad transformed travel over the whole of North America. No longer was ready access to a body of water a prerequisite for good transportation. Communities across the country grew on the strength of a railroad stop, and competition between communities increasingly focused on the acquisition of one or more railway lines.

These three transportation forms (turnpikes, canals, and railroads) share several key characteristics. In none of them did planners design a national system. Instead, a national system developed as local communities, state and provincial governments, and private enterprises connected smaller pieces of the network into a whole. This move from local to national systems is illustrated in the wide range of gauges used in railroad lines by 1870. The adoption of a standard gauge made it possible for the first time to move cars from one railroad line to another. And only in the case of the railroad can we honestly speak of a national network in the United States. The advent of the railroad preempted attempts to create national transportation networks based either on canals or turnpikes or both.

Railroads were initially developed in much the same way as turnpikes and canals, with a combination of public and private funds. Up until 1828, the federal government had on occasion invested directly in transportation improvements. After Andrew Jackson's presidency, however, federal involvement was indirect—primarily through the land grants. State and local governments generally followed this same pattern—buying stock and donating the land rather than owning it. U.S. railroads benefitted substantially from these public subsidies, receiving over 130 million acres of land from the public weal (almost 10 percent of all the land in the United States).

Winnipeg, Manitoba As with the engineers who constructed the first generation of canals in North America, the earliest railroad engineers learned on the job. One of the most prominent railroad engineers in Canada, Henry Norlande Ruttan certainly fits this description. Ruttan was born in 1848 in Cobourg, Ontario. As Norman Ball explains:

> Like many engineers of the day, Ruttan seems to have bypassed college. Engineering was learned on the job and after a stint in military life beginning at age 16, he joined the Chief Engineer's Department of the Grand Trunk Railway in 1868. Here he worked with and learned from E. P. Hannaford, one of the great Canadian civil engineers of the day. Ruttan next worked with another of the greats in Canadian engineering history, Sir Sandford Fleming, who was then building the Intercolonial railway from Quebec to the Atlantic seaboard. Soon Ruttan found himself on the biggest Canadian engineering project of the day—building the Canadian Pacific Railway (CPR). From 1874 to 1876 he headed the location party between the Rocky Mountains and Edmonton. He spent three years as contractor's engineer on construction work between Winnipeg and the Lake of Bays. Next he was engineer in charge of building the CPR section from Rat Portage, now Kenora, to Cross Lake. This pattern of increasing responsibility on larger jobs was followed by his decision to strike out on his own. . . . Ruttan's experience and character made him an excellent choice for Winnipeg's first City Engineer. He served from 1885 to 1914.

Source: Norman Ball, "People in Public Works—Henry Norlande Ruttan," *APWA Reporter* (June 1987): 4–5.

In the case of all three of these forms of transportation, then, the decisions made within a local area regarding improvements carried weight. Communities committed scarce financial resources to a form of transportation that would advance their interests. Local historians can learn much about this era through a careful study of these decisions. Who within the community advocated transportation improvements? Which ones? Did transportation improvements precede or follow periods of economic and population growth for a community? How were the required funds raised? Did capital come from inside or outside the area? Did anyone oppose transportation improvement? Who and why?

The development of airports in the twentieth century fit much this same pattern. Local initiative led to the first airports in the years around World War I, and until 1930 less than half of the airports in the United States were publicly owned. In some communities, private enterprise and/or local government combined to build airports for a budding new transportation form after the First World War. The strategic military importance of airports became clear in the interwar period. By the end of the Second World War, the federal government made money available for the development of airports, so long as local communities were willing to negotiate the planning and building process and provide some of the necessary funding. Between 1946 and 1971, the federal government spent $1.2 billion on airports, largely in the form of grants to local governments.

From the rise of the railroad until the early twentieth century, there were few attempts to develop good roads over long distances. This began to change with the introduction of the automobile. In North Carolina, Harriet M. Berry was responsible for rallying support to the cause of good roads in the years just before and after the First World War. In 1921, the *Raleigh Times* noted that she was: "willing and able to furnish actual, usable information on anything connected with the roads of the State, [and] to her more than any one person or groups of persons is due the thanks of those who desire to bring North Carolina out of the mud."

Berry was born in Hillsborough, North Carolina, in 1877. After college, she joined the staff of the North Carolina State Geological and Economic Survey. Miss Hattie, as she was known, was instrumental in organizing the North Carolina Good Roads Association in 1902, which lobbied for a state highway system. She enlisted grassroot support for her proposals, traveling across the state. One newspapers described her as "the best woman politician in the state." By 1921, passage of a state highway act was a foregone conclusion, and Miss Hattie could take much of the credit.

North Carolina historian Jeffrey J. Crow explains her role:

> The good roads movement in North Carolina, coming as it did near the climax of the Progressive era, dramatized the shift from local funding and control to state financing and responsibility for roads and road building. It also represented government's growing professionalism and expertise in dealing with social and economic problems too large and too complicated for the local community or governmental unit to cope with effectively. But in the end it took the determination and dedication of one woman to galvanize the campaign for good roads. Berry's successful fight probably cost her her job, for she lost her post with the state Geological and Economic Survey in 1921. Later she returned to public service to help organize credit unions and savings and loan associations throughout the state before her retirement in 1937. When she died in 1940, few questioned her accolade as North Carolina's "Mother of Good Roads."

Source: Jeffrey J. Crow, "People in Public Works—Harriet M. Berry," *APWA Reporter* (November 1977): 4–5.

In the 1920s and 1930s, airplanes attracted great crowds for special events. This 1936 aerial photograph shows the original Los Angeles airport terminal during the National Air Races. The terminal was on the south side of the field. Of particular interest are the thousands of cars along with the crowds of people which were present around the airport. *Courtesy of the Public Works Historical Society of the American Public Works Association, Kansas City, Missouri.*

The people who built public works across North America
are often not familiar faces. However, local public works or
highway departments often have photographs on file which
help researchers in constructing profiles of these figures.
Douglas B. Fugate was one of those engineers instrumental
in constructing the state highway system in Virginia. *Cour-*
tesy of the Public Works Historical Society of the American
Public Works Association, Kansas City, Missouri.

In the twentieth century, better roads and the emergence of the
automobile began a slow shift back to roads and highways. Local and
state governments took the lead—by 1940, California's freeways and
Pennsylvania's turnpike were the first modern limited-access highways. The 1916 Federal Aid Road Act began subsidies for designated
federal highways. The 1956 Interstate Highway Act further shifted the
burden of funding to the federal level in the United States. Ninety percent of funds for the construction of the interstate highway system

came from the federal government. As with airports, the strategic military importance of highways helps to explain this funding shift.

The interstate highway system was a marked departure for other reasons as well. Centrally planned and directed, local initiative was largely limited to setting specific paths for the interstate through a community. Even here, state highway departments exerted the strongest control. In exploring the local component of the interstate highway system, local historians most often face the task of looking at the ways in which a single community responded to a system imposed from afar.

While the federal government provided most of the funds for the Interstate Highway System and set its general path, state highway departments bore the responsibility for planning, constructing, and maintaining the system within their jurisdiction. Douglas B. Fugate directed much of this work in Virginia, where he eventually served as Comissioner of the Virginia Department of Highways and Transportation.

Fugate was born in 1906 and trained as a civil engineer at Virginia Military Institute. Although his family lived only ninety miles from the Institute, he was only rarely able to visit because of the poor, unpaved roads. After graduation, Fugate went to work for the Virginia Department of Highways. In 1956, he was named coordinator of Virginia's share of the Interstate highway system. In this position, he supervised surveys, plans, construction, and eventually maintenance of the system.

In 1964, Fugate convinced the government and general assembly that the state should develop a 1,750 mile arterial highway network to "supplement the interstate system and serve areas which would not be served directly by an interstate route. This arterial program extended modern highways to every community with a population of 5,000 or more."

Source: Howard Rosen, "People in Public Works—Douglas B. Fugate," *APWA Reporter* (April 1989): 24–25.

WATER RECLAMATION

Each of these transportation networks has left its mark on communities across the country. Historians are interested in exploring the ways in which local residents financed, built, and administered these

Across the Southwest, irrigation systems have been the responsibility of local communities for thousands of years. While massive federal projects dwarf these small irrigation systems, they remain a crucial part of life in the southwest. Here El Cerrito, New Mexico, citizens work on their community irrigation system. *Courtesy of the Bureau of Agricultural Economics, Washington, D.C.*

networks, and the ways in which the networks in turn affected the lives of local residents.

Transportation networks are by no means the only public works that tie individual communities to a wider region. Water reclamation is another infrastructure system whose influence is particularly strong in the western part of the United States. As Ellis Armstrong, Michael Robinson, and Suellen Hoy explain in *History of Public Works in the United States*,

> In many ways, irrigation played the major role in the growth and development of the western half of the United States. It furnished the means for making areas of the West suitable for settlement and created a fron-

tier where people could find opportunity for economic betterment. Vital centers of the West owe their very existence primarily to irrigation and in a large measure, to those irrigation public works provided with federal government assistance. Included among these centers are the Salt Lake City area of Utah; the Rio Grande Valley of Colorado, New Mexico, and Texas; the Phoenix area of Arizona; the Central Valley of California; the Boise Valley of Idaho; the Yuma, Imperial, and Coachella Valleys of Arizona and California; the Yakima Valley and the Columbia River Basin in Washington; and the North Platte River Valley of Wyoming and Nebraska. Without irrigation, little would have happened in these areas and public works have been key to stable irrigation development. (p. 303)

Phoenix, Arizona In the area which today comprises the western United States, irrigation has been practiced for millenia. For instance, more than 700 years ago the Hohokam Indians constructed an elaborate system of canals to bring water to their crops. In the Salt River Valley, "[u]sing only stone and wooden tools, they created one of the earliest American reclamation projects—more than 150 miles of canals, enough to irrigate thousands of acres of land." While the Hohokam vanished by 1400, they left behind a network of river valleys.

Hundreds of years later, when American settlers came to the area (in and around present-day Phoenix), they found the evidence of this early irrigation system and used this knowledge in their own efforts to bring water to their crops and livestock. One early settler, engineer and surveyor William A. Hancock, "established lines and grades for several of the valley canals" which provided water to farmers by the 1870s. Hancock worked for

> reclamation projects in the Salt River Valley and elsewhere: He fought tirelessly on behalf of reclamation, writing many letters to Representative Francis Newlands, an author of the proposed national reclamation law then before Congress. Hancock urged Newlands to continue his fight for the Reclamation Act, although it faced bitter opposition from eastern and midwestern interests who argued against federal support of the West at the expense of eastern farmers. Western reclamationists were also divided among themselves over the question of federal assistance versus private development. Hancock was not opposed to federal aid for irrigation and water storage, although he favored local initiative and popular control.

Source: Christine Lewis, "People in Public Works—William A. Hancock," *APWA Reporter* (March 1986): 4–5.

As a result of reclamation programs that date back to the late nineteenth century, many western communities rely on large-scale public works for water. At first private and state efforts, then federal reclamation projects made farming and community life possible in the Far West. Massive dam, canal, aqueduct, and irrigation projects are a visible reminder of this network, particularly in California and the Southwest. Many of these projects remain under the direction of federal agencies. A 1969 survey of all water supplied through irrigation in the United States found that nearly 40 percent came from Bureau of Reclamation projects.

Las Vegas, Nevada Perhaps no public works project is as dramatic as that involving the Colorado River. Michael C. Robinson has explored these developments in *Water for the West: The Bureau of Reclamation, 1902– 1977*. Robinson noted that the Colorado River drains parts of seven states (some 250,000 square miles), comprising almost one-twelfth of the land area in the continental United States. Private efforts to divert water from the Colorado into California's Imperial Valley date back to the 1890s. In 1928, the federal government began construction on what would later be known as the Hoover Dam. Robinson explains:

> Hoover Dam was perhaps the most significant American public works project of the twentieth century. It was the first large Federal conservation undertaking based on multiple-purpose objectives. The dam transformed the economy of the Southwest, provided water and power for rapid growth in southern California, and paved the way for Grand Coulee, Shasta, Glen Canyon, and other great dams. The 726-foot-high structure, nearly twice as high as any then existing dam, became a symbol of pride and accomplishment during a period of national despair. (p. 51)

The Hoover Dam and related projects provided water for agricultural lands in the Imperial Valley of California. The water diverted through the project also solved the critical water shortages faced by residents of Los Angeles. Thirteen southern California cities formed the Metropolitan Water District of Southern California in 1931 and built the Colorado River Aqueduct to supply water to their communities.

Local historians should be aware of wide networks of public works projects that can deliver water for farming and community needs. While local water sources provide for the needs of many communities, other local areas use water drawn hundreds of miles from home. Basic questions which can uncover these connections, include: What is the source of water? How far is that source from the community? How does water get from this source to the community? What agency oversees the movement of water? While aqueducts, canals, and dams are most often associated with agricultural projects, they play an important role in the water supply systems for many cities, including New York, San Francisco, and Boston.

The large scale of many reclamation projects in the United States has led to considerable federal involvement. In 1902, Congress organized the Reclamation Service, under the direction of Frederick H. Newell. The Reclamation Service investigated seventy-nine irrigable areas across the West between 1902 and 1907 and completed twenty-five reclamation projects based on these surveys. As Michael C. Robinson explains,

> Reclamation built many types of public works to store, divert, and transmit irrigation water to arid lands. Water supplies of rivers and natural lakes were sometimes utilized, and in many cases dams were built across canyons to store spring floodflows for irrigation during the summer growing season. Constructing monumental masonry and concrete storage dams was the Service's stellar achievement. The agency pioneered designs and construction methods and assembled an outstanding public works organization.

The Bureau of Reclamation's projects have made it possible for many communities and farms to exist in areas which could not naturally support such intensive habitation.

Source: Michael C. Robinson, *Water for the West: The Bureau of Reclamation, 1902–1977* (Chicago: Public Works Historical Society, 1977).

Related to reclamation projects, such as that involving Hoover Dam, is another service network: electricity. Water at dam sites can be used to generate electricity, and in the case of federal reclamation projects from the middle of the twentieth century, this became a means of financing the entire public work. Since 1936, the Hoover Dam project has supplied water and power to the Los Angeles Metropolitan area. Congress created the Tennessee Valley Authority (TVA) in 1933 with a multipurpose agenda: flood control, economic development, navigation improvements, and hydroelectric projects. The TVA began selling electricity in its first year of operation; and Tupelo, Mississippi, be-

The work of the Bureau of Reclamation has dramatically reshaped the landscape of the western United States over the course of the twentieth century. Shown here is the Arrowrock Dam in Boise, Idaho, taken from high on the hillside and showing the spillway running full. *Courtesy of the Bureau of Reclamation, Pacific Northwest Region, Boise, Idaho.*

came the first community in the region to buy it. Rates dropped almost by half for most customers, and the number of residential customers increased by 30 percent. Across the Tennessee Valley, local communities extended electric service as a result of larger, regional networks of hydroelectric power.

Local historians exploring local history must look at the connections that a single community has to wider networks. Power, water, flood control, and transportation are but a few of the ways in which local communities are tied to regional and national networks of public works. These networks serve as reminders that local history is played out on a regional, national, or even international stage.

SUGGESTED READINGS

At the outset, it is important to note that while public buildings are indeed public works and part of the infrastructure, they are not considered in great detail in this volume. See Gerald Danzer, *Public Places: Exploring Their History* (Nashville: American Association for State and Local History, 1987). See also Ronald E. Butchart, *Local Schools: Exploring Their History* (Nashville: American Association for State and Local History, 1986) for information on the physical structures of schools.

For general discussion on each of these kinds of infrastructures, see Armstrong, Robinson, and Hoy, *History of Public Works in the United States, 1776–1976* (Chicago: American Public Works Association, 1976); and *Building Canada: A History of Public Works* (University of Toronto Press, 1988). *The Public Historian* reviews recent books related to irrigation, water, and electricity, especially in the West.

For information on the early age of turnpikes, see George Rogers Taylor, *The Transportation Revolution, 1815–1860* (New York, 1951). Other sources on highway developments in the United States include: Bruce Seely, *Building the American Highway System* (Philadelphia: Temple University Press, 1987); Marilyn E. Weigold, "Pioneering in Parks and Parkways: Westchester County, New York, 1895–1945," *Essays in Public Works History*, 9 (1980); David W. Jones, Jr. *California's Freeway Era in Historical Perspective* (Berkeley: Institute of Transportation Studies, University of California, 1989); Joseph Durrenberger, *Turnpikes: A Study of the Toll Road Movement in the Middle Atlantic States and Maryland* (Cos Cobb, CT, 1968); Edwin C. Guillet, *The Story of Canadian Roads* (Toronto, 1960); and Mark Rose, *Interstate: Express Highway Politics, 1941–1956* (Lawrence, KS: University of Kansas Press, 1979). See also *An Interview with Ellis S. Armstrong* (Chicago: Public Works Historical

Society, 1988). Armstrong was a federal highway official during the height of the interstate highway program. For a more regional focus: Carl Abbott, "The Plank Road Enthusiasm in the Antebellum Middle West," *Indiana Magazine of History*, 63 (June 1971): 95–116 and Emory L. and Janet Kemp, "Building the Weston and Gauley Bridge Turnpike," *West Virginia History*, XLI (Summer 1980): 299–332.

Sources on the canal era include: Carter Goodrich, ed., *Canals and American Economic Development* (Port Washington, NY, 1960); Goodrich, *Government Promotion of American Canals and Railroads, 1800–1890* (New York, 1960); John Lamb, *I & M Canal: A Corridor in Time* (Romeoville, IL: Lewis University, 1987); Jack Gieck, *A Photo Album of Ohio's Canal Era, 1825–1913* (Kent, OH, 1988); Ralph D. Gray, *The National Waterway: A History of the Chesapeake and Delaware Canal, 1769–1985* (Champaign: University of Illinois, 1989); Robert Leggett, *The Ottawa River Canals* (Toronto: University of Toronto Press, 1988); and Robert W. Passfield, *Canals of Canada* (Vancouver, 1976).

The American Canal and Transportation Center has an extensive list of publications, including ones that focus on canals in Pennsylvania, Ohio, and the Chesapeake region. For more information write American Canal and Transportation Society, 809 Rathton Road, York, PA 17403.

History of Public Works in the United States, pp. 131–159, provides an overview of railroad history. See also Carl Condit, *The Railroad and the City: A Technological and Urbanistic History of Cincinnati* (Columbus: Ohio State University Press, 1977); *ibid.*, *The Port of New York: A History of the Rail and Terminal System from the Beginnings to Pennsylvania Station* (Chicago: University of Chicago Press, 1980); and *ibid.*, *American Building* (Chicago: University of Chicago Press, 1968). See also Roger Grant and Charles Bohi, *The Country Railway Station in America* (Pruett Publishing, 1978). For historical information on the development of airports, see Paul Barrett, "Cities and Their Airports: Policy Formation, 1926–1952," *Journal of Urban History* 14 (November 1987): 112–37; Ellimore Chanpie, *The Federal Turnaround on Aid To Airports, 1926–1938* (Washington, DC, 1973); Nich Kommons, *Turbulence Aloft* (Washington, DC, 1976); and Dorothy Nelkins, *Jetport* (Boston, 1974).

For a general discussion on American bridge history see Donald C. Jackson, *Great American Bridges and Dams* (Washington, DC, 1988). Jackson includes a bibliography of recent work on the history of bridges, including state surveys.

Michael C. Robinson, *Water for the West: The Bureau of Reclamation 1902–1977* (Chicago: Public Works Historical Society, 1982) provides an excellent overview of western water policy. See also William Kahrl,

Water and Power (Berkeley: University of California Press, 1982); Donald J. Pisani, *From Family Farm to Agribusiness: The Irrigation Crusade in California and the West, 1850-1931* (Berkeley: University of California Press, 1984) and William K. Jones, "Los Angeles Aqueduct: A Search for Water," *Journal of the West*, 16 (July 1977): 5-22. For a closer look at one of the Bureau's larger projects see also Joseph Stevens, *Hoover Dam* (Norman, OK: University of Oklahoma Press, 1988). Eugene P. Moehring discusses the effect which the construction of Hoover Dam had on Las Vegas in *Resort City in the Sunbelt: Las Vegas, 1930-1970* (Reno, University of Nevada, 1989).

For a longer view of water in one state see Ira Clark, *Water in New Mexico: A History of Its Management and Use* (Albuquerque, University of New Mexico, 1988). David L. Nass, "Public Policy and Public Works: Niagra Falls Redevelopment as a Case Study," *Essays in Public Works History*, 7 (1979) provides information on a large-scale water project in the East.

PART III

FINANCIERS, BUILDERS, AND USERS

Chapter 6

GOVERNMENT AND FINANCE

Historical research is not only useful to understanding the development of utilities and public services (and their future directions), but also to fathoming elusive concepts such as community. This chapter will plumb the interrelationships between community, local governments, and finance with regard to public services and local utilities. Local historians may find here ways to connect and explain trends within their communities.

Infrastructure networks are very often extremely expensive. In fact, the very idea of a community can in some sense be equated with that group of individuals willing to share the cost of constructing something for the public good, a public work. Of course, this definition means that the idea of community is not static, but ever changing. A group of individuals who form a community changes over time and circumstances. Local historians have the opportunity to explore these shifting boundaries by examining the basic question: who pays for an improvement and who benefits?

Answers to this two-pronged question lead inevitably to government. Governments are the conduits for community action. Individuals who come together to develop a service or public works turn to government—or create a governmental unit—to execute their aims.

As outlined in Chapter 3, there is not a simple ratio of one government to one locality. In the example of Sacramento, literally hundreds of governments provide services in Sacramento County. The various governments which provide services are layered one on top another over a particular geographic area.

Today, governmental units regulate or provide most utilities and services. It is important to see that many governments were in fact created specifically to plan, build, and administer public works. Governmental units have not only been responsive to constituent demands for services, but some have actually been created by that demand.

Governmental units closely connected to a specific service are special districts. Special districts have been created in urban and rural communities to provide services as diverse as water, roads, sewers, mosquito abatement, or libraries. These districts are defined geographically and provide one specific service to a constituency which at its inception saw itself as a community with regard to at least one issue. Farmers organized irrigation districts across the West in the early twentieth century to take advantage of water from larger reclamation projects. In the United States, these districts, often encompassing thousands and thousands of acres of agricultural land, have broad financial, planning, management, and operational responsibilities.

The Ohio River Valley Water Sanitation Commission (ORSANCO) is one of the largest special districts in the United States. Organized in 1948, the ORSANCO consists of three representatives from the federal government and three members from each of its member states—Ohio, West Virginia, Virginia, Illinois, Indiana, Kentucky, New York, and Pennsylvania. The mission of the ORSANCO was to promote regional water pollution control. Similar special districts, organized to manage water or waste, are found in many North American communities.

Chicago, Illinois The Metropolitan Water Reclamation District of Greater Chicago (MWRDGC) protects the drinking water and manages the wastewater for over 11 million people in the Chicago metropolitan area. Organized in 1889, the MWRDGC began its protection of the quality of drinking water by reversing the flow of local rivers (filled with raw sewage) away from Lake Michigan. The district completed the reversal project between 1892 and 1900 at a cost of approximately $35 million. Frank E. Dalton, MWRDGC general superintendent, explains that this project:

> was regarded as one of the [world's] monumental engineering achievements. The construction techniques and key supervisors on this project later went to Panama and built the Panama Canal. Books have been written on, not only the construction of the Sanitary and Ship Canal, but the legal battles that followed dealing with the diversion of Lake Michigan water into the Mississippi watershed. At the time the canal opened [1900], the area was permitted to use 10,000 cubic feet per second of diversion water. The problem of deaths from waterborne disease was stopped and the population grew.

By the 1970s, the MWRDGC embarked on another project to protect the Chicago Metropolitan region from the ill-effects of raw sewage. All fifty-two member communities, as well as other public bodies in the Chicago metropolitan area, adopted an ambitious regional flood control plan. The Tunnel and Reservoir Plan includes the collection of excess rainwater in a series of underground reservoirs, making it one of the largest public works projects ever undertaken.

Source: Frank E. Dalton, "Public Involvement and Public Support in the Urban Water Management Field," in *Water and the City: The Next Century,* Howard Rosen and Ann Durkin Keating, eds. (Chicago: Public Works Historical Society, 1991): 3–8.

In contrast to special districts created to provide a specific service, chartered municipalities—and counties—were existing governmental forms which during the nineteenth century were called upon to provide and regulate a broad range of services. Up until the mid-nineteenth century, the primary function of municipal governments was to foster trade—the basis of urban economies in a mercantile economy. To this end, municipalities maintained infrastructure improvements that fostered trade, such as markets, docks, and street paving.

With the advent of industrialism, urban residents called on municipal governments to provide a wider range of services. Not only did municipalities foster commerce, but increasingly sought to protect the health and promote the public order within their growing communities. Joel A. Tarr and Josef W. Konvitz explain this development in their essay "Patterns in the Development of the Urban Infrastructure":

> Structural changes in city government permitted the development of the service orientation, as states granted municipalities new charters and authorized the revision of old ones. By the 1840s and 1850s, in larger municipalities, functions such as firefighting had been assumed by professional fire departments; organized police forces had taken the place of the night watch and constables; and urban governments had enlarged their activities in matters involving public health and sanitation. (In Howard Gillette, Jr. and Zane L. Miller, *American Urbanism: A Historiographical Review* (New York: Greenwood Press, 1987): 197)

Among the public health and sanitation initiatives that many municipalities undertook for the first time during the nineteenth century were water supply, sewerage, garbage disposal, and street cleaning. In

Remembering to keep people in the story of infrastructure improvements is important. Politicians, engineers, and local residents all are involved in this process. Decisions about public works improvements are often made by town councils or boards. Shown here is the Irwin, Iowa, town council meeting (with the municipal library along the walls). *Courtesy of the Bureau of Agricultural Economics, Washington, D.C.*

addition, urban governments regulated other public services and utilities such as street railways, gas companies, and electric franchises.

Houston, Texas Houston grew in the nineteenth century as a result of the westward movement of the population of the United States and the success of Houston boosters in building a city which attracted commerce and industry. Over time, residents called on Houston's municipal government to provide or regulate many service improvements and utilities. Historian Harold Platt has written about Houston's growth and explains:

> Beginning in the 1840s, the provision of public services played an increasingly important role in defining the issues of municipal politics. City builders

first voiced demands for paved streets, pure water supplies, artificial illumi-
nates, and horsecar lines as community requirements, vital to public health
and commercial enterprise. Only the rich could initially afford the luxury
of installing plumbing and gas lighting in their homes. Gradually, however,
more and more city dwellers came to regard modern amenities as individual
as well as collective necessities of urban life. The resulting formation of
neighborhood groups around calls for service extensions and improvements
gave ward level politics a life of its own, independent from traditional party
affiliations.

A comparison of Houston's municipal expenditures in 1866 with 1901
shows a dramatic expansion in municipal function and expenditures.
Houston's city government added the following functions from 1866 to
1901: health, utilities, education, sanitation, and recreation. At the same
time, expenditures rose from $88,239 to $580,000.

Source: Harold Platt, *City Building in the New South: The Growth of Public Services in Houston, Texas, 1830–1915* (Philadelphia: Temple University Press, 1983),
p. xvi.

An interesting issue raised by this evolution of municipal government is the connection between community and public works. Unlike
a special district, formed to maintain one specific service to a clearly
defined constituency, municipalities have expanded from their original functions, and their constituencies have changed dramatically. Bit-
ter disputes between different groups in a city often result in stale-
mates on the provision of public works, services, or utilities. This is
true as much for today as it was one hundred years ago. Who pays for
an improvement and who benefits are difficult questions, particularly
in the context of large heterogeneous urban areas.

Charlottetown, Prince Edward Island Disputes over services are often
resolved in the political arena. For example, the City Council of Charlottetown, Prince Edward Island, spent decades developing a sewerage system
which met both the expectations and the pocketbooks of its constituents.
Beginning in the late 1860s, the Municipal Health Officer, Dr. Richard
Jenkins, made public connections between contaminated well water and
diseases like typhoid and cholera. Jenkins fought to close contaminated
wells and for the creation of a sewerage system to avoid more groundwater contamination.

However, it was not until the late 1880s that the City Council seriously considered the construction of a sewer system. And it was not until 1897 that construction began. As historian Douglas Baldwin explains:

> Few people opposed the principle of sewerage, provided that it was commensurate with their means. Many taxpayers, however, believed that the city's modest resources did not warrant the enormous outlay needed for a proper sewage system and were not willing to pay higher taxes. Equally important, advocated had not yet convinced the population of the necessity of sewerage.

In 1897, a plebiscite on the sewerage issue found the majority of residents in favor of constructing a sewer system, although there was no agreement on its method. Some, including engineering consultant George E. Waring, favored the least costly method of discharging the untreated sewage directly into the harbor. Others, including Richard Jenkins, advocated the creation of sewage farms, where human wastes could be returned to the soil as fertilizer. The final decision was to go with the less costly alternative, dumping sewage into the adjacent harbor.

Although completed in 1898, it was decades before the majority of homes in Charlottetown were connected to the sewerage system. The ten-dollar connection fee, as well as the cost of installing plumbing within existing homes, "meant that cesspools and filthy steets remained a public health menace." By the 1920s, considerable new housing (which by municipal regulation had to connect to the sewerage system) finally brought a citywide system.

Source: Douglas Baldwin, "Sewerage," in *Building Canada: A History of Public Works* (Toronto: University of Toronto Press, 1988): 227–230.

City governments are not the only governments providing a wide range of services within a metropolitan area. Since the end of the last century, suburban governments have maintained public works for the benefit of their constituencies. Initially, suburban communities were places where residents sought to combine rural life with the amenities of city living. Real estate developers promoted subdivisions on the outskirts of major cities with the lure of amenities such as transportation, water, sewers, schools, and streets.

While providing many of the same improvements as larger municipalities, suburban governments generally service a far more homogeneous constituency. This homogeneity often results in far more consensus regarding which improvements to make and how much to spend on them.

Private developers had their hand in early infrastructure improvements in many suburban areas across North America. In the late nineteenth century, developer Sam Brown, Jr., marketed a subdivision just south of Rogers Park in Chicago which he called the Sheridan Drive Subdivision. This photograph shows some of the basic infrastructure improvements which Brown provided privately to attract purchasers to his development: graded (and some paved) streets, sidewalks, streetlights, and shade trees. The history of many neighborhoods and suburbs begins with a similar enterprise. *Courtesy of the Sulzer Branch, Chicago Public Libraries, Chicago, Illinois.*

While local historians can explore the background of the multitude of governments with jurisdiction within any community, it is important to note that some governments, which may have been quite important to the provisions of services and utilities in the past, no longer exist.

For example, in many urban areas, annexations have led to the expansion of territory under the control of a municipal government. In some cases, governments disappeared as a result of an annexation. The most spectacular annexation in the United States was the 1898 consolidation of Brooklyn and New York City, which ended Brooklyn's existence as an independent government. More typical were annexations of smaller suburban communities to city center. For instance, the villages of Somerville and Roxbury annexed to Boston, Rogers Park and Lake View to Chicago, and Mount Vernon to New York City, in the closing years of the last century. At the time of their annexation, each had already begun to provide service improvements to their residents.

Rogers Park is today the neighborhood in the far northern reaches of the City of Chicago along Lake Michigan. However, Rogers Park began its history as an independent village, located along a railroad line north of contiguous urban settlement. In 1872, the Rogers Park Land Company opened and graded streets and began selling lots in its subdivision beside a commuter stop of the Northwestern Railroad. After a few more years, residents banded together to form a village government that began to lay the groundwork for infrastructure networks.

By the early 1890s, the village government of Rogers Park provided such basic improvements as sewers, paved streets, electric lights, and gas mains. A private company sold water to village residents, and boosters claimed that the waterworks was one of the best of its capacity in the state. However, these services could not compare with the large scale water and sewer works of Chicago. In 1893, residents of Rogers Park voted to join the city, in hopes of receiving better services at a lower cost.

Though Rogers Park residents had hoped for quick improvements in basic services after annexation, they soon found that their work had only begun. Residents organized the Rogers Park Improvement Association at the turn of the century, which had to lobby hard before finally receiving connections to the city's water, sewer, and electric systems in the first decade of the twentieth century.

Source: Ann Durkin Keating, *Building Chicago: Suburban Developers and the Creation of a Divided Metropolis* (Columbus: Ohio State University Press, 1988).

Local government, in a variety of forms, maintains public services for its residents. As has been the case for other facets of public works research, historians know the most about the largest systems. What is not as well known, and in many cases not known at all, is how these functional changes affected small and medium-sized communities. Local historians can provide the information to expand discussion beyond the largest cities.

While the forms of local government and the functions which they perform are critical to understanding who pays and who benefits from public works, the ways in which these projects are financed are also important. There are some basic categories for financing public works projects. Among the methods are: general funds, user fees, special assessments, special taxes, bonds, or private funds. These funds can come from private sources or from local, state, or federal governments. It is not unusual to find an infrastructure system financed by a combination of these methods. For instance, residents in many nineteenth century cities funded waterworks using some combination of bonds, general funds, and user fees. This in part reflected a notion that a waterworks provided general community benefits (and so the general funds), benefits for future residents (and so the bonds), as well as benefits to the individual household that tapped into the system (and so the user fees).

General funding is the basic tool of government finance. Most simply, general funds are those derived from broad-based taxes. Up until the early twentieth century, these taxes were primarily on real estate at a local level and tariffs on trade goods at a federal level. Just before the First World War, the income tax began to emerge as the principal source of federal funds. These taxes are not, however, dedicated to specific projects when they are collected. Instead, the use of these monies is identified at the discretion of public officials. In a real sense, projects financed with general funds reflect a wide view of community and the body politic. In theory, everyone pays, but everyone benefits. General taxes also reflect a "pay as you go" philosophy—building only what the tax base can support at a particular point in time.

Atlanta, Georgia While the theory behind general taxes is that everyone pays and everyone benefits equally, in reality those with greater power within a community have often received more than their share of services. For instance, historian Howard L. Preston has explored the inequality in services received for taxes paid in metropolitan Atlanta,

Georgia, between 1900 and 1930. Preston found that residents within the city limits, one-third of whom were African-American, subsidized schools, highways, sewers, and health programs in suburban areas.

This disparity was in part the result of revenues being collected by one local government, Fulton County, but used by many—including the City of Atlanta and suburban governments and by Fulton County on behalf of unincorporated areas. Underlying this complex governmental situation, however, is the fact that socioeconomic power can, and does, distort the equality of government expenditures.

Source: The description of Preston's work is taken from Kenneth T. Jackson, *Crabgrass Frontier: The Suburbanization of the United States* (New York: Oxford University Press, 1985): 132.

Special taxes are also a way to fund a specific public works project. Generally used for one-time expenditures, these taxes are levied over and above regular taxes for a specific purpose—whether building a bridge, school, or water pumping station. The purpose of the tax is generally clearly delineated and the whole community is taxed for the improvements, not some special subset (making for a special assessment, not a special tax).

Bonds are a quite different approach to financing. In this case, a governmental body decides that an improvement—whether it be a sewer system, a street, or a new school—will benefit not only those individuals currently living in the community, but those who will reside there in the future. Therefore, bonds (essentially loans taken by local governments that it will repay at some definite point in the future) reflect the notion that public works construction has a lasting benefit. To a certain degree, bonds allow current residents to have the benefit of an improvement, while sharing its cost with future residents. Of course, the same individuals often comprise a community today and in the near-term future.

For instance, during the early nineteenth century, residents of New York City encountered a serious shortage of clean water for household use. In 1832, 3,500 people died in a cholera epidemic, which led many to work for a new water source. Adding more impetus to their quest was an 1835 fire that destroyed over 500 businesses. Because of the clear need for an adequate water supply, engineers designed an aqueduct system that brought water to New York City from the Croton River, forty miles north of the city. The plans were dramatic and expensive, estimated to cost five million dollars. The state legislature passed enabling legislation to allow the city to float an extensive bond

Reservoirs are an important feature of water supply systems in many communities. Providing a place to store water for use as needed, reservoir systems help to protect communities from shortages. This drawing shows a bird's eye view of the Lake Manhatta and the Old Reservoir located in Central Park in 1869. *Courtesy of the Public Works Historical Society of the American Public Works Association, Kansas City, Missouri.*

issue, but the citizens of New York City had to approve the bond issue as well. Seventy-four percent of the voters did so and gave the city government the power to float the necessary bonds. The final cost for the project was seven million dollars over the original estimate of five million dollars. The extra cost helped to set New York on course for financial disaster in the 1870s.

When completed in 1849, the system included a five-mile long dam, over forty miles of aqueduct, and a thirty-five acre reservoir in Central Park. While the builders of the Croton felt it would adequately supply water to New York City for at least thirty years, by the 1860s expansion was already required. All of the pipe that conveyed water across the Harlem River was replaced with larger-diameter pipe, to increase daily capacity. Other expansion projects continued almost unabated into the twentieth century.

Sometimes a community construes the beneficiaries of a public works project as a much narrower group than all residents. In this case, special assessments are levied only on those parts of a community who are deemed to have received benefits from the improvement. Special assessments have often been used for secondary street and sidewalk improvements—where the benefits are seen to largely derive to the abutting property owners. In this case, the local government simply acts as an administrator of the project.

Chicago, Illinois The Chicago city government gained the power to levy special assessments for street paving from abutting property owners in its initial 1837 charter. When residents on a specific block petitioned the city government for street paving, the city took bids on the work from private contractors. Once the cost had been determined, it was divided up among the abutting property holders, according the street frontage. In this way, the city supervised street paving without using any general funds.

Some commentators were critical of government involvement in the process. After the 1871 Chicago fire, the *Chicago Tribune* called for paving streets by private contract. A September 5, 1875, editorial summarized the lengthy assessment process as follows: first the city council appoints three aldermen as a commission to report on the cost of the improvement; then the council orders a petition filed in court for proceedings to assess property owners; then the court appoints three commissioners "to ascertain the comparative value of the improvement to contiguous property and assess it accordingly; an assessment role is made and returned to court; assessment notices are sent to all assessed; if no one objects in court after a prescribed period of time the improvement is made; if there was an objection then a formal jury trial was held and the jury made the assessment (with the possibility of an appeal to the Supreme Court)." *The Tribune* concluded its editorial: "It will be readily inferred from this description of the length of legal red tape required for paving streets by special assessment that it is utterly impracticable in a large city like this, and particularly when so many of the streets should be paved immediately."

Many of the street improvements made in the years following were done through private contracts. The Department of Public Works found fault with this alternative to special assessments as well. In the department's 1877 annual report, it was noted that:

> the system of paving streets by private contract, which has been largely carried out since the great fire, will, from all appearances, be abandoned in a great measure, and the old system of letting contracts to the lowest respon-

sible bidder be reinstated. The reason being that property owners are beginning to discover that this is the much cheaper and better plan, and the contractors finding it so difficult to collect their bills when there is no lien on the property.

Along a similar line are users fees. In this case, individuals who wish a service must pay a specified fee. Rather than having free access to the service—whether it is water or highways or some other improvement—community residents must decide whether they want to bear an additional cost. As with special assessments, users fees often indicate that a community sees the service as more a benefit to an individual or household than to the community at large. At the same time, the general provision of the service may be deemed a public good, so long as those individuals who have access to the service pay the full cost—or perhaps an additional amount beyond a community-wide investment.

Freeways Versus Tollways During the 1930s, state highway departments across the United States tried varying methods to fund the construction of the first limited access automobile highways. Engineers worked from the model of the German Reich Autobahnen to design highway systems in California, Pennsylvania, New York, and other states. In eastern states such as Pennsylvania, turnpikes were opened in the years just before and after the Second World War. These turnpikes were planned and built by special state authorities, which sold bonds that were to be retired with toll revenue from the turnpikes.

In contrast, Californians financed their highway development with a gasoline tax. Their roads were soon known as "freeways" in contrast to the eastern toll roads. In the early 1950s, when federal officials were debating the form of the interstate highway system, they worked from these two very distinctive models of highway financing. Influenced by the precedents set in Pennsylvania and California, the federal government opted to finance much of the interstate system with a Highway Trust Fund based on specific motor-vehicle user taxes (i.e., gasoline tax, heavy-vehicle tax).

Source: Mark H. Rose, *Interstate: Express Highway Politics, 1941–1956* (Lawrence: Regents Press of Kansas, 1979).

An aerial view of an interchange on the New York Thruway is a familiar image to Americans at the close of the twentieth century. The creation of thousands of miles of limited-access highways across Canada and the United States since 1945 is one of the most dramatic public works of recent history. Highly charged public debates often accompanied decisions about the location of expressway interchanges, as the relative value of land and businesses rose or fell on these decisions. *Courtesy of the Public Works Historical Society of the American Public Works Association, Kansas City, Missouri.*

Users fees are related to the fees that private service providers charge residents for utilities like telephone, gas, and electric service. Instead of a community-owned enterprise, though, the basic system is privately held. When the infrastructure network is seen as essential to the working of a community, local governments often regulate the private utility through franchise agreements. While government is not providing the service outright, it is regulating its provision.

Of course, a single person or a group of individuals may band together to provide a service privately. That is, a group of residents may come together to build a water system, pave a street, or construct a sewer on their own. This is generally only possible in rural areas, outside the bounds of local governments who might wish to regulate their actions. Real estate developers are sometimes among this group—installing a series of improvements that will increase the value of lots in a subdivision to attract potential purchasers. Eventually, improvements made in this way can be integrated into public systems.

Private development of infrastructure points up the fact that services and improvements, which a contemporary identifies as "public works," may have changed over time and probably will continue to change. As noted at the beginning of this chapter, municipalities dramatically expanded their functions during the second half of the nineteenth century. Up until that time, municipal governments had only slowly begun to widen their constituencies beyond the merchants and businessmen who controlled their economies. Street improvements, waterworks, and sewerage systems became integral parts of municipal business. When studying financing, or other aspects of infrastructure construction, it is important to consider the public or private origins of the project.

State and provincial government involvement in the provision of public works has expanded over the last 150 years. Such governments helped to finance or actually build canals, toll roads, railroads, and public buildings during the nineteenth century. In the twentieth century, state and provincial governments have overseen the construction of highway networks linking communities within a state and across the whole of North America.

There has been an ebb and flow to federal involvement in infrastructure projects both within and between communities in the United States. From the 1791 construction of Cape Henry Lighthouse in Virginia, federal involvement in public works has evolved. During the nineteenth century, the federal presence was felt most strongly in a move towards internal improvements under the direction of the U.S. Army Corps of Engineers. The Corps of Engineers supervised projects as diverse as harbor improvements and federal buildings. Federal land grants underwrote much of the railroad expansion in the United States. In the twentieth century, and particularly since the New Deal, the federal government has provided funding for a wide variety of community public works projects including sewer systems, waterworks, and highway development.

These funding decisions are all made within the political arena. That is, decisions to make improvements and how they will be funded are an important part of the story which local historians can capture by returning to town or city council minutes or newspaper coverage of debates about making infrastructure improvements. No history of a particular public works system would be complete without an exploration of the discussion preceding funding and construction of a specific improvement.

Perhaps the most famous political debate about an infrastructure improvement dates back to the presidency of Andrew Jackson. The federal government had during the first decades of the nineteenth century provided funding for canal and road projects as well as for harbor improvements. Federal lands had been granted for turnpike development in Ohio and Indiana, and in 1830 Kentucky sought funding for the Maysville Turnpike. Andrew Jackson vetoed the funding legislation, because it was not a national or general road, but instead was wholly within the state of Kentucky. Jackson felt that because it was essentially a local improvement, the whole population of the United States should not be forced to provide the requested subsidy.

When discussing financial issues related to infrastructure networks, it is also important to note that the costs of infrastructure systems do not end with construction. Once infrastructure systems are in place, they must be maintained. Local historians can chronicle the ongoing debate on where maintenance funds are to come from. The high initial cost of infrastructure systems makes it imperative that maintenance be funded, but the less glamourous nature of maintenance and repairs leads historians and the public to slight this area of concern. Other questions which local historians might consider investigating regarding the interrelationships of government, finance, and public works include: How homogeneous or heterogeneous is the constituency for a governmental unit? What effect does this have on the form of financing?

SUGGESTED READINGS

Financing infrastructure networks is an area in which much historical work is yet to be done. Two historians who have pioneered work in this area are Heywood T. Sanders and Terrence McDonald. Sanders has studied bonding in Cleveland; see "Voters and Urban Capital Finance: The Case of the Disappearing Bond Election," an unpublished paper presented at the annual meeting of the American Political Science Association, San Francisco, September 1990. McDonald explored financing San Francisco's city government. See *The Parameters of Urban Fiscal Policy* (Berkeley: University of California Press, 1986).

There are several sources on private development of infrastructure networks—or the work of real estate developers in the development process. See essays by Eugene P. Moehring and Ann Durkin Keating in "Infrastructure and Urban Growth in the Nineteenth Century," *Essays in Public Works History*, 14 (1985). See also Eugene P. Moehring, *Public Works and the Patterns of Urban Real Estate Growth in Manhattan, 1835–1894* (New York: Arno Press, 1981) and Ann Durkin Keating, *Building Chicago: Suburban Developers and the Creation of a Divided Metropolis* (Columbus: Ohio State University Press, 1988). Marc A. Weiss also has done considerable work in this area, including *The Rise of the Community Builders: The American Real Estate Industry and Urban Land Planning* (New York: Columbia University Press, 1988). And on the issue of public or private provision of services, see "Privatization: Public-Private Partnerships in Historical Perspective," *Essays in Public Works History*, 16 (1990).

Robin Einhorn has done interesting new work on the use of special assessments for street improvements in nineteenth-century Chicago. See *Property Rules: Political Economy in Chicago, 1833–1872* (Chicago: University of Chicago Press, 1991). See also Carl V. Harris, *Political Power in Birmingham, 1971–1921* (Knoxville: University of Tennessee Press, 1977); Terrence J. McDonald and Sally K. Ward, eds. *The Politics of Urban Fiscal Policy* (Beverly Hills: Sage Publications, 1984); Alan D. Anderson, *The Origin and Resolution of an Urban Crisis: Baltimore, 1890–1930* (Baltimore: Johns Hopkins University Press, 1977); and J. Rogers Hollingsworth and Ellen Jane Hollingsworth, *Dimensions in Urban History: Historical and Social Science Perspectives on Middle-Sized American Cities* (Madison: University of Wisconsin Press, 1979).

Chapter 7

BUILDERS BEHIND
THE NETWORKS

Because infrastructure systems are so often invisible to the general public, the individuals who conceive, design, construct, and maintain them are often neglected. Yet these people are critical to the modern life of every community resident. The engineers and workers who are responsible for these improvements provide an important area of investigation for local historians interested in public works. Public works professionals are often overlooked as leaders by local histories. They remain a largely unexplored group within community history. Adding these individuals to a community's history becomes an important task for local historians.

Of course, some of the men who designed key infrastructure systems in the United States are familiar historical figures. Benjamin Henry Latrobe was perhaps the most famous American engineer working in the eighteenth century. Latrobe trained in England and Germany, combining both a classical education with practical work performed under the guidance of prominent British architects and engineers. After Latrobe arrived in the United States, he was responsible for a number of important public works projects, including the Philadelphia waterworks (1799–1801), a drainage system for Washington, D.C. (1815–1816), and the United States Capitol and the White House.

In the twentieth century, Robert Moses became a prominent figure during his thirty-year career in New York City. Moses was involved in a wide range of projects in the New York metropolitan area between the 1930 and 1970. They included seven major bridges, expressways, numerous city and state parks (Moses expanded the number of city playgrounds from 119 to 777), two world's fairs, Shea Stadium, thousands of public housing units, and reclamation projects that added

Robert Moses directed the development of many of the massive public works projects in the New York metropolitan area in the twentieth century, without ever
having to stand in a public election. Here he poses looking over the St. Lawrence
Seaway while it was still under construction in the early 1950s. *Courtesy of the
Power Authority of the State of New York, Albany, New York.*

over 15,000 new acres to New York City along its river and ocean
fronts.

Albert Edward Berry, whose career in Ontario covered much the
same time as Moses' in New York City, gave service and leadership in
many fields including: water supply, sanitation, pollution control,
water resources, and conservation. As Director of the Sanitary Engineering Division of the Ontario Department of Health in the 1930s and
1940s, Berry supervised all water and sewerage work in the province.
He championed the chlorination of water, arguing that it ranked with
the introduction of compulsory pasteurization of milk as a contribution to public health. From 1956 to 1963, Berry directed the Ontario

Water Resources Commission, which became internationally known for its research efforts.

Meadville, Pennsylvania While Labtrobe, Moses, and Berry were prominent individuals, well known outside their profession, many of the leaders in public works are far less visible. They spend their lifetimes in service to one community, and their efforts are rarely acknowledged. One such individual was Roy L. Phillips.

Phillips served as city engineer in Meadville, Pennsylvania, from 1918 to 1957. Trained as a civil engineer, Phillips worked for just a few years as a consulting engineer before taking his post with the City of Meadville. Phillips oversaw many, many projects. In all of them, he followed this view: "We must get away from the foolish idea that we must have everything all at once and be willing to set aside funds from year to year to provide cash for the construction of specific improvements which we are sure will be needed. We must be willing to do our bit for posterity in exchange for the good things which we in turn inherit from our ancestors."

Robert R. Perry, of the Water Pollution Control Federation, described Phillips's career in Meadville:

> In 1918 much of the city was unsewered and only 14 miles of the streets were paved. By 1957 most of the streets and alleys had been paved and the sewerage system served the entire community. . . . When the primary treatment plant was placed in operation in 1933 it was debt free, a feat few cities could claim today even with 75% federal funding. A mono hearth incinerator was also constructed after World War II. . . .
>
> During the 1940s and 1950s, when asphalt became the common pavement for urban streets and asphalt resurfacing of brick streets seemed the "modern" practice for cities, Phillips resisted. He felt that brick pavements, if properly maintained, would far outlast asphalt. And perhaps more important, he could see the beauty in a well-constructed brick pavement. . . .
>
> Phillips was also unique in that he had an intense interest in music. He played the flute in the community band until his death and was a member of a woodwind quartet which performed simply for its own pleasure. . . . Philllips represented a type of public servant and a style of life that we are again beginning to appreciate. He enjoyed the life he had made for himself in Meadville—one fabricated from an intense commitment to his profession and his community. Roy Phillips looked upon it as a labor of love. It is doubtful that he ever considered a job in another location.

There is no monument to Roy Phillips in Meadville, nothing that bears his name as testament to his years of service. At his death, though, one of his associates noted: "It is not possible to name any municipal improvement that was made between 1918 and 1956 that was not inspired by the city engineer and in most instances the plans were actually drawn by Roy L. Phillips."

Source: Robert R. Perry, "People in Public Works—Roy L. Phillips," *APWA Reporter* (March 1981): 4–5.

Most public works engineers, architects, and administrators are far less well known. Many work the whole of their careers largely shielded from the public eye because they are not elected officials. But the influence that they have on our lives can be profound.

While it is important to focus on the engineers who designed and administered public works projects, the vast majority of individuals involved in building public works projects have been—and continue to be—the corps of workers who actually build and maintain public works. Unlike engineers or administrators, however, few of the names of these individuals are readily available to historians. The gangs of workers who constructed railroads and canals across the United States, or sewer and water systems, are important but anonymous parts of local history.

Today, when we consider massive public works projects, we assume that they were planned and constructed by highly trained engineers and constructed by a skilled labor force. Certainly this has been the rule for the whole of the twentieth century. However, many infrastructure systems date back to the nineteenth and even the eighteenth century. The engineers who designed them were often practically trained, and the men who actually built early public works often had no special skills or talents. During the colonial era, local residents banded together to build and maintain basic public works like roads and bridges. Well into the nineteenth century, rural residents built and maintained their own roads. There were no distinctive "public works" laborers. Instead, every household had to provide a certain number of days of labor towards the maintenance of roads (and often bridges and any public buildings as well). This system operated without monetary taxes and with limited oversight.

The British North American colonies directed the construction and maintenance of basic roads, which linked inland settlements with the Atlantic Coast. How were these roads financed and who actually labored on them? William S. Price, Jr., Director, Division of Archives and History of the North Carolina Museum of History, explores these questions for North Carolina:

> Leaders in North Carolina naturally modeled their early road building system on what they were already familiar with—that is, the ways roads had been built in the "mother country" England. As early as 1555 an English law provided that each "householder" in a parish (a local unit smaller than a modern county) must work four days a year to maintain roads and bridges within its boundaries. . . .
>
> Not only were the outlines of the English system transferred to North Carolina, but the requirements were even harder. The earliest road law that exists for North Carolina was written in 1715, but it was based on a law that had existed many years earlier—perhaps as early as 1670. The law passed by the North Carolina General Assembly in 1715 required that certain males between the ages of sixteen and sixty work on building and maintaining roads and bridges in their precincts (after 1738 precincts became counties). The number of days per year that such free labor had to be performed was not specified until 1771 when a law provided that no one would be required to work on roads more than twelve days a year!
>
> . . . A particularly hateful aspect of the road-building system in early North Carolina was the way in which certain people were exempted or excused from having to work on roads. Members of the legislature, court judges, coroners, constables, clergymen, attorneys, clerks of the court, physicians, persons tending public ferries, and schoolteachers were not required to work on roads. Also anyone who provided three people to work in his place could be excused. Those three substitutes were usually servants or slaves, and after 1756 only slaves could serve as substitutes. . . . Therefore unpaid labor on the roads of early North Carolina was performed by lower-class whites, white and black indentured servants and black slaves.

Source: William S. Price, Jr. "Free Roads? Road Building in Colonial North Carolina," *Tar Heel Junior Historian* (Winter 1984): 5–6.

Many nineteenth-century American civil engineers gained their training on huge public works projects like the Erie Canal and the railroad projects. They then went on to design new urban infrastructure systems in large and small cities. For instance, John B. Jervis gained a practical engineering education in the early nineteenth century through his eight years of work on the Erie Canal as an axeman, rodman, stone-weigher, and surveyor. Jervis then went on to serve as the chief engineer of New York's Croton and Boston's Cochituate aqueducts. One of Jervis's assistants on the Boston waterworks in the 1840s was Ellis S. Chesbrough, who like Jervis had begun his career on western transportation projects. After working with Jervis in Boston, Chesbrough became that city's first city engineer and later became chief engineer of Chicago's sewerage system.

Workers on the Erie Canal, the Brooklyn Bridge, the railroad, and water and sewer projects were often drawn from the ever-growing pools of immigrant labor available during the nineteenth century. Skilled craftsmen, such as ironworkers and brickmasons, as well as unskilled laborers were paid for their labors on these projects. There is still relatively little known about these people who labored long and arduous hours to construct projects which still today provide the basis for our infrastructure.

Brooklyn, New York Among the most visible and endearing public works projects from the nineteenth century is the Brooklyn Bridge, which crosses the East River linking Manhattan with Brooklyn. Under the careful of guidance of John A. Roebling and his son Washington A. Roebling, the bridge, begun in 1869, was completed fourteen years later. The bridge took a serious toll from these supervising engineers. The senior Roebling died of tetanus after a ferryboat crushed his foot, and his son was afflicted by caissons disease—the bends—from his many trips down into the pneumatic caissons used to build the below-water structure.

While the Roeblings' story is well known, the efforts of the thousands of workers who toiled to make this bridge a reality are not. At least twenty-three deaths and hundreds of injuries came during the years of bridge constrution. David McCullough, in his book, *The Great Bridge: The Epic Story of the Building of the Brooklyn Bridge*, provides readers with more information than is generally available about workers who build public works projects.

One of the most dangerous parts of the project was done in the caisson (which was a gigantic box filled with compressed air, resting on the river bottom). Men worked eight-hour shifts on the river bottom, even staying below to eat their dinners. Their pay increased as the caisson reached more deeply into the river bed. Many workers quit because of the bad air and potentially hazardous working conditions. But scores of European immigrants were eager to earn the relatively high wages paid to caisson workers.

Very few first-hand accounts of the workers have been found. Frank Harris, an Irish immigrant, wrote of his experiences in the caisson:

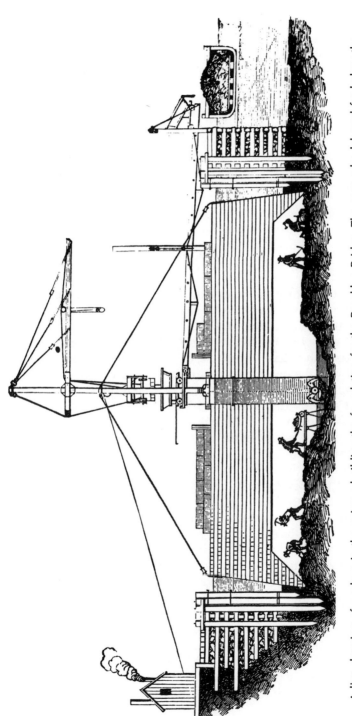

A line drawing of workers in the caisson building the foundation for the Brooklyn Bridge. The men who labored far below the river's surface were subject not only to bad air and cramped working conditions, but to the diver's disease, the bends. *Courtesy of the Public Works Historical Society of the American Public Works Association, Kansas City, Missouri.*

When we went into the "air-lock" and they turned on one air-cock after another of compressed air, the men put their hands to their ears and I soon imitated them, for the pain was acute. Indeed, the drums of the ears are often driven in and burst if the compressed air is brought in too quickly. . . . When the air was fully compressed, the door of the air-lock opened at a touch and we all went down to work with pick and shovel on the gravelly bottom. My headaches soon became acute. The six of us were working naked to the waist in a small iron chamber with a temperature of about 80 degree Fahrenheit: in five minutes the sweat was pouring from us, and all the while we were standing in icy water that was only kept from rising by the terrific pressure.

Source: David McCullough, *The Great Bridge: The Epic Story of the Building of the Brooklyn Bridge* (New York: Simon and Schuster, 1972), p. 302.

Over the course of the nineteenth century, professional training became more and more common for engineers responsible for designing, constructing, and maintaining public works. At the time of the Civil War, only a few institutions, such as West Point, Rennsselaer Polytechnic Institute, and Stevens Institute, offered engineering training. After the Civil War, the number of institutions providing engineering education expanded rapidly. Many of the new land-grant universities, including Cornell, Illinois, and Michigan State became leaders in engineering education. By 1880, there were eighty-five schools where engineering was taught in the United States (as compared with only four in 1840).

By the 1880s, the growing number of university-trained engineers supported the development of the American Society of Civil Engineers. Engineers joined together in many communities across the country to create local clubs—the Boston Society of Civil Engineers, begun in 1848, is the oldest such group in the United States. Often local historians can find out who the principal actors were in infrastructure building by examining the records of local societies such as these.

Smaller communities were unable to support full-time design engineers. Instead, they called in consulting engineers to design and construct systems. This was a common scenario regarding water and sewer systems in the late nineteenth century, when engineers with expertise in these areas consulted in communities across North America. George Waring visited both U.S. and Canadian cities in the late nineteenth century (including Charlottetown, Prince Edward Island), advising community leaders about the design of sewerage systems.

Workers found danger not only in the caisson far below the surface of the river, but also in the construction of the upper parts of the Brooklyn Bridge. This photograph show the foot bridge, part of the suspended span, the main cables, and the floor beams of the bridge. *Courtesy of the Public Works Historical Society of the American Public Works Association, Kansas City, Missouri.*

Ellis S. Chesbrough, while serving as Chicago city engineer during the 1860s and 1870s, also accepted consulting assignments on water supply systems for Pittsburgh, Detroit, and Toronto and sewer systems for Milwaukee, New Haven, and Indianapolis.

Engineering expertise not only assisted the development of better infrastructure design and systems, it also played an important role in improving the equipment which workers used to create and maintain systems. For instance, up until the twentieth century, road building was back-breaking work done by hand by gangs of men (and as seen from the North Carolina example, some of this was forced labor). By the mid-1920s the Fresno scraper had revolutionized this work. Pulled by several horses, it looked something like a snow shovel that could haul dirt off a highway path. This early labor-saving machine was the forerunner of the enormous self-loading scrapers used in highway construction today.

Fighting Creek, Idaho The efforts of thousands of workers created the roads across North America. Norman Best was a highway worker in the 1920s in Idaho, Washington, Oregon, and Montana. In his reminiscence, *A Celebration of Life,* Best describes the early highway building in the Northwest. He remembers that many of the highway crews were composed of local farmers, looking for extra income. They took the work to earn extra income, and used their own horse teams:

> The equipment for the job was rudimentary but effective. In construction language it would be called a horse and Fresno outfit. A Fresno is a giant version of a scoop shovel (like a snow shovel), designed to be pulled by several horses. . . . Moving dirt with a Fresno was not easy; the teamster walked along behind the horses all day long in a big circle, loading up, hauling out to the fill, dumping the load, and going back for another. That made for a long, arduous day, yet there were no complaints; those men were good to work with. On that job the horses established the rhythm of work, so they were allowed to set their own pace and were rested sufficiently to last the day. In some ways the horses were treated with more consideration than the workers in the woodyard.

Source: Norman Best, *A Celebration of Work* (Lincoln: University of Nebraska Press, 1990).

During the 1930s, the federal government initiated and funded a wide range of public works programs in local areas across the United

States. Many of these program were aimed at putting people to work doing worthwhile projects. Thousands of public works projects were completed under the aegis of the Public Works Administration (PWA), the Works Progress Administration (WPA), and the Federal Works Authority. Post offices, government offices, schools, bridges, roads, sewage treatment plants, and parks were among the projects funded by the federal government during these years. In the main, these projects were planned, built, and administered by local authorities, with at least partial funding from the federal government.

Another program, the Civilian Conservation Corps (CCC), was established in 1933 to put unemployed men between the ages of eighteen and twenty-five to work. The program was abolished in 1942, with World War II already underway. These young, unmarried men had to enroll for a minimum of six months. They were paid a stipend of thirty dollars a month, but had to send twenty-five dollars of that amount home to their needy families. Beginning in 1933 individual states organized CCC Camps, run like a military unit. These young men were put to work at various projects, depending on local requirements. Some worked on roads, some developed parks and recreational structures, while others were involved in cleanup efforts.

Fort Bragg, North Carolina In North Carolina, at least sixty of the one hundred counties had one or more CCC camps within their boundaries during the 1930s. Enlistees began with two weeks of conditioning and training at Fort Bragg, and then were assigned to a specific camp. Historian Harley E. Jolley describes their work:

> For most, camp life was a new and exciting experience. Practically everything, from the food to social life and work, contained a new challenge, adventure, or opportunity. One lad, writing to his mother, said, "Mom, you won't believe the food they give us. One of the things they feed us is yellow looking, round, and about a quarter of an inch thick, and umm-mm, it was good. They call it a pine-apple, I think."
>
> . . . With good food came work assignments. By 1937 North Carolina had sixty separate camps serving about fifty counties and nine agencies, including the United States Forest Service, the Soil Conservation Service, State Forest Service, the Tennessee Valley Authority, and private lands. From the mountains to the seashore, a remarkable variety of tasks were tackled and the results are still being enjoyed today. These included the construction of recreational facilities, reforestation, erosion control, timber-stand improvement, firebreaks, beach stabilization, as well as construction of trails, roads, and bridges. Most of the state parks, the Great Smoky Mountains National Park, the Pisgah National Forest, the entire shoreline of North Carolina, and

During the 1920s, trucks began to replace teams of horses on highway crews. These highway construction workers were driving a Waterloo Boy tractor and road scraper in 1920. *Courtesy of Deere & Company, Moline, Illinois, and the Public Works Historical Society of the American Public Works Association, Kansas City, Missouri.*

By the 1950s, scrapers and graders were more elaborate. Cabs protected highway workers from the elements and larger wheels aided in smoother operations. This photograph was taken on a road construction job near Yuma, Colorado, in July 1951. *Courtesy of the Public Works Historical Society of the American Public Works Association, Kansas City, Missouri.*

143

thousands of acres of private land received the healing touch of their labor. And, in addition, some $82 million were pumped into the North Carolina economy during the lifetime of the program.

Source: Harley E. Jolley, "Hard Times and Happy Days: The Civilian Conservation Corps in North Carolina," *Tar Heel Junior Historian* (Winter 1984): 18–21.

One group of public works engineers who have influenced most communities across the United States since World War I is state highway engineers. They were responsible for the construction and maintenance of roads across each state, and during this period they were also responsible for the construction of the Interstate Highway System within the boundaries of their respective states. The expressways and interstate routes, which today we take so much for granted, were sited and designed by these largely faceless men (there were virtually no women engineers involved in this process—although women like Harriet M. Berry were involved in fighting for better roads).

In 1956, the federal government began the Interstate Highway Program to construct 41,000 miles of roads that would link the United States with one comprehensive transportation system. Though the federal government raised most of the funds, determined the general routes, and set road standards, state highway departments actually constructed the interstate system. State engineers determined specific routes, where interchanges would be located, and the timing of the improvements. These engineers were required to appear at public hearings on these issues, and it is here that community opposition was most often raised. The Interstate Highway Program affected thousands of communities across the United States—by linking some more tightly to others, by physically dividing or destroying parts of them, and by shifting the center of growth toward the interstate route.

Sacramento, California The Public Works Historical Society in Chicago recently completed an Interstate Highway Project for the American Association of State Highway and Transportation Officials (AASHTO). The project included interviews with over one hundred state officials who were involved in building the interstate system.

The interviews covered a wide range of topics, from construction techniques to environmental concerns. George A. Hill, who worked for the California Department of Transportation, discussed the issue of routes and rights-of-way. This is the point at which the planned routes of highway planners confront the real world—where land for the highways must be taken away from other uses:

> What they were supposed to do [in right-of-way acquisition] was to go in and talk to the people and lay out that this was the freeway route that had been [adopted] by the highway commission, the legislature had established the route and we had gone through the public hearing process. . . . there was considerable publicity given where we made an effort to get the newspaper coverage that we could and whatever cooperation we got from them and the other media—the TV or the radio.

At these meetings, engineers explained why they needed the right-of-way and the condemnation proceedings. Hill opined that the appraisals for condemned homes were

> quite generous. Not only did we give the whole market value of their house, but we went some little extra. It was always determined they would get sufficient funds to go out and buy the equivalent place in an equivalent neighborhood in the same area and that was the basis for the appraisal.

For more information about specific engineers and their interviews, contact the Public Works Historical Society, 106 W. 11th Street, Kansas City, MO 64105-1806.

Local historians can research the development of recent projects such as the Interstate Highway Program through resources as diverse as records of public hearings, newspaper reports, and interviews with participants. Engineers who worked on community projects often have a great deal to add to our understanding of the rationale and original intent of public works. Interviews and biographical research into the individuals who planned and built these systems also remind historians that people, not structures, are at the center of the story.

Not only the engineers, but the workers are important parts of these stories. Historians have yet to answer many basic questions about those who labored to construct public buildings and services: Where did these workers come from? Where did they live? Did they stay in the community after construction was completed? These are among the many as-yet unanswered questions about the individuals who actually built the infrastructure networks on which our modern lives depend.

SUGGESTED READINGS

Public works equipment is explored in *One Hundred Years of Public Works Equipment: An Illustrated History* (Chicago: Public Works Historical Society, 1986). This and other books published by the Public Works Historical Society are available from its office at 106 W. 11th Street, Kansas City, MO 64105-1806. The reminiscence of Norman Best is entitled *A Celebration of Work* (University of Nebraska Press, 1990).

The history of civil engineering is explored in several volumes. See David P. Billington, *The Town and the Bridge: The New Art of Structural Engineering* (Princeton: Princeton University Press, 1983); Daniel C. Calhoun, *The American Civil Engineer: Origins and Conflict* (Cambridge: MIT Press, 1960); and Raymond H. Merritt, *Engineering in American Society, 1850–1875* (Lexington: University Press of Kentucky, 1969). Specific information on the Brooklyn Bridge is drawn from David McCullough, *The Great Bridge: The Epic Story of the Building of the Brooklyn Bridge* (New York: Simon and Schuster, 1972).

A number of prominent engineers who designed infrastructure systems are the subjects of biographical accounts. See Edward C. Carter II, "Benjamin Henry Latrobe and Public Works: Professionalism, Private Interest, and Public Policy in the Age of Jefferson," *Essays in Public Works History*, 3 (1976); Louis P. Cain, "Raising and Watering a City: Ellis Sylvester Chesbrough and Chicago's First Sanitation System," *Technology and Culture* 13 (July 1972): 353–72; Martin V. Melosi, "Pragmatic Environmentalist: Sanitary Engineer George E. Waring, Jr.," *Essays in Public Works History*, 4 (1977); Larry D. Lankton, "The 'Practicable' Engineer: John B. Jervis and the Old Croton Aqueduct," *Essays in Public Works History*, 5 (1978) and Robert Caro, *The Power Broker: Robert Moses and the Fall of New York*.

The Public Works Historical Society also publishes a series of oral histories with leading figures in the field of public works history. Interviews include Jean Vincenz, Samuel A. Greeley, Samuel S. Baxter, Edward J. Cleary, William D. Hurst, Jennings Randolph, and Ellis L. Armstrong. These are available from the Public Works Historical Society.

In researching the background of civil engineers in any part of the United States, consult the American Society of Civil Engineers, *A Biographical Dictionary of American Civil Engineers* (New York: American Society of Civil Engineers, 1972).

Chapter 8

HOMES AND INFRASTRUCTURE NETWORKS

Much of what is known today as public works history is about highly educated white men: the engineers, consultants, and politicians who planned, financed, and administered public works and infrastructure projects. Of course, a great many more people are involved in this history. Previous sections of this volume have raised other ways of approaching public works history which would include more groups: exploring those who labored on, as well as those who designed, projects; looking at smaller communities; and examining "who pays for and who gets" improvements.

Another important way to expand public works and infrastructure history is to examine public works from the perspective of the household. In the household, the historical role of women in public works becomes clear. Women adapted household chores to take advantage of the growing number of improvements available. It was women who directed the transformation of daily life wrought by new services and infrastructure.

Up until the mid-nineteenth century, most households provided water, waste disposal, power, heat, and light for their members without much help from the wider community. Women, men, and children labored within homes that were physically separated from one another. The only infrastructure connections were streets, which made travel between homes and businesses possible. One historian, David P. Handlin, noted in his book *The American Home* that "Many of the machines that found their way into American homes at the end of the nineteenth century were attached to power and service lines. Water pipes, electrical cables, sewage systems, telephone lines, hot-air ducts, and gas mains were manifestations of progress. . . . They disrupted age-old re-

While women did work on public works construction projects before the 1964 Civil Rights Act, they were few in number. Here a 1918 survey party composed entirely of women works in Minidoka, Idaho. *Courtesy of the Public Works Historical Society of the American Public Works Association, Kansas City, Missouri.*

lationships and brought people in contact with one another in ways that they were not accustomed to or did not understand."

Lawrence Experimental Station, Massachusetts In 1887, the Massachusetts Board of Health founded the Lawrence Experimental Station, which pioneered an interdisciplinary approach to public health problems. Young engineers, chemists, and biologists came together at the station to solve some of the thorniest problems related to water purification and sewage treatment techniques. Chemist Ellen Richards was among them.

By 1900, Richards, then a researcher at the Massachusetts Institute of Technology, turned her attention to related public health problems within homes. She estimated that a house costing $5,000 in 1850 cost as much as $20,000 by 1900 due to the "increased sanitary requirements" and "the finish and fittings" demanded in good homes. In the twentieth century, the automobile and the computer have dramatically changed the lives of Americans. Analogously, in the nineteenth century these infrastructure improvements did the same thing. They also provided a similar disruption and uncertainty about the future. In the late nineteenth century, homes were connected to outside networks in new and disconcerting ways. Ellen Richards thought perhaps this foretold near-constant changes in the shape and fitting of homes, so much so that she concluded that "our houses in America are mere extensions of clothes; they are not built for the next generation. Our needs change so rapidly that it is not desirable." Richards wasn't much of a fortuneteller, but her comments do reflect the revolutionary changes that took place during her lifetime.

Source: Ann Durkin Keating, *Building Chicago: Suburban Developers and the Creation of a Divided Metropolis* (Columbus: Ohio State University Press, 1988).

Books published by and for architects, tradesmen, builders, and home economists chronicle the changes that took place within American homes. Carpenters and builders relied heavily on pattern books to create housing in the late nineteenth century. By then, patterns books devoted considerable attention to the placement of plumbing and other infrastructure connections. Home economists at the turn of the century wrote about the proper care and upkeep of these systems. One 1878 home economics manual discussed water, drainage, heating, lighting, and ventilation in separate chapters.

Plumbers played a vital role in the introduction of service improvements into homes across North America. At the beginning of the nineteenth century, plumbing was barely an occupation. Metal-working craftsmen created any number of specialized pipe or metal items needed in homes or businesses. As the nineteenth century unfolded, plumbers emerged from the ranks of more general craftsmen to cater to the specialized needs of water, sewer, and gas systems. At first, they made their own fittings and installed them. By 1900, though, plumbers seldom manufactured their own materials, working almost exclusively with fittings.

To keep up with the changes, a master plumbers' associations was organized nationwide in 1880. The association kept its members abreast of the latest changes in plumbing technology and engineering. City and suburban governments began to license plumbers in order to regulate the installation of sewer, water, and gas pipes within the city. This served as further acknowledgment of the complexity of the work of plumbers and its growing importance to public health.

Debates concerning the "best" construction methods, designs, and fixtures for water, sewer, gas, and electric improvements made the work of plumbers challenging. The plumber in many cases was called on to advise home builders. One Chicago master plumber in 1880 explained that a plumber "should stand in the same relation to his customer as the family doctor does to his patient—that is as an advisor." By the turn of the century, many homeowners were convinced that "the plumbing is the most important work that is put into a building."

How did daily life change because of service connections into a home? To many, the obvious answer is that it reduced work—or at least made it easier. This certainly appears to be the case. Running water allowed for the introduction of stationary baths, kitchen sinks, laundry tubs, and other innovative uses. For the first time, household members were freed from the backbreaking work of hauling water from an outside source into the home, and also from carrying water to the various parts of the home where it was desired. Tasks such as laundry could be done within the home with greater ease. Households adjacent to sewerage systems could abandon their backyard privies and install water closets with indoor plumbing. Backyards no longer served as dumping grounds for waste and could be used for gardens and other recreational purposes.

However, this simple answer masks another trend which accompanied the reduction in work on specific household tasks. Historian Ruth Schwartz Cowan identified this trend in her book *More Work for Mother*: "As the nineteenth century wore on, in almost every aspect of household work, industrialization served to eliminate the work that

In the late nineteenth century, when many infrastructure connections were first being made to homes and businesses in communities across North America, work took place both inside and outside of buildings. Here, telephone and electric lines are fully visible, while workers uncover underground infrastructure systems. *Courtesy of the Public Works Historical Society of the American Public Works Association, Kansas City, Missouri.*

men (and children) had once been assigned to do, while at the same time leaving the work of women either untouched or even augmented." For instance, the introduction of piped water into a household meant that children no longer hauled water from a nearby well or stream. However, women continued to clean house, cook, and wash clothing with this water. A new gas stove meant that men no longer corded and carried wood into the home for cooking, which was still primarily done by women. Connections to public services and utilities changed work, eliminating many onerous tasks, but it seldom actually reduced the work of women within a household.

Milford, Massachusetts Many changes took place within middle class households in the first decades of this century. Ruth Schwartz Cowan provides a sense of this with her description of the changing household of L. R. and Maria Dodge. L. R. Dodge was a conductor on the New Haven and Hartford Railroad. He and Maria Dodge were married in 1889 and had three children between 1892 and 1899. They lived in a single-family home in Milford, Massachusetts. Cowan describes the ways in which Maria Dodge's life was changed by service improvements:

> Early in her marriage, such a housewife probably cooked on a coal or a wood-burning stove and lighted her house with gas or kerosene lamps. If she lived in a city, she probably had running water in her house, but she may still have been heating it in a reservoir attached to her stove; if she lived in a town, she might still be pumping water from a well in her yard. Some time after the turn of the century, however, various improvements were made to her property which both increased its value and altered the pattern of her work. The Dodges installed a bathroom in their house in 1904. . . . [and] connected their house to the gas mains in Milford in 1913 and purchased a range for the kitchen at the same time. . . . The Dodges were "wired" in 1914, at a cost of $15.50 for electric fixtures, $2.50 for a transformer, and $24.00 for a vacuum cleaner . . . Irons, vacuum cleaners, and fans were fairly common appliances which comfortable people acquired soon after installing electricity for lighting; washing machines and refrigerators had not yet made their appearance.

Source: Ruth Schwartz Cowan, *More Work for Mother: The Ironies of Household Technology from the Open Hearth to the Microwave* (New York: Basic Books, 1983): 155–56.

By the turn of the twentieth century, running water was a standard feature of urban households. Even the poorest families generally had access to a water tap in the building where they lived. However, it was not until the middle of the twentieth century that appliances such as hot water heaters, showers, and bathtubs became common items. Until then, women still heated and carried water around the house. Not until the post-World War II housing boom did most homes boast these appliances.

Gas connections transformed other aspects of life within a home.

Until the introduction of gaslighting, homes were poorly lit by candles and lanterns. Gaslight dramatically increased the activities which could take place within an average home after sundown. After the widespread introduction of electricity for lighting urban households in the early twentieth century, gas companies successfully championed appliances such as gas stoves, hot water heaters, and hot air furnaces, which maintained their connections to many households. By 1930 gas cooking was the most prevalent form, and gas space and water heating were popular.

Electricity affected daily life over the course of several decades. Developed by Edison in the 1880s, by 1907 only 8 percent of households in the United States had electric connections. By 1920, over one-third of the households in the country were wired for electricity. Initially, electricity was used almost exclusively for lighting. Electric lights were far cleaner than gas fixtures, and this was the primary reasons for an electric connection until the First World War.

During the 1920s, the price of sewing machines, washing machines, refrigerators, and vacuum cleaners dropped as mass-production techniques were introduced. With the aid of rural electrification programs during the 1930s, the number of households in the United States with electrical connections rose to 80 percent, with electric irons to 79 percent, 52 percent had washing machines and refrigerators, and 47 percent had vacuum cleaners. All of these changed the ways in which household work was accomplished, although they did not necessarily reduce household work.

Water pipes for running water, sewer hookups for indoor plumbing, gas and electric fittings for lighting and appliances, and telephones for direct communication beyond the home revolutionized both domestic life and its connections to the outside world. Homes became more intimately and physically attached to the world around them, largely through new underground utility networks. Homeowners came to rely on local governments and utilities for their everyday routines.

A survey of the connections between a house and the community provides physical evidence of the links between homes and their wider communities. Infrastructure connections are visible in basements or crawl spaces. Scan the exterior walls of the basement for pipes or conduits that appear to leave or enter the building. Water pipes, sewer lines, gas and electric connections, and telephone lines often run initially from the basement through the rest of a house. Sometimes a rough sketch of the lines identified helps to sort through the different services.

Moving outside, try to connect the lines found inside the home with

By the mid-twentieth century, homes within many communities boasted several infrastructure connections: water, sewers, electricity, telephone, and gas lines. In addition, sidewalks and streets visibly linked homes through public works. In 1940 new sidewalks were evident on a residential street in Irwin, Iowa. *Courtesy of the Bureau of Agricultural Economics, Washington, D.C.*

those outside. Phone and electric lines can be clearly visible, as they are often connected to utility poles. Gas lines can sometimes be identified because of attached meters. In contrast, there are often no visible signs of sewer and water connections outside the home, as these infrastructure connections are buried underground.

In addition to these functioning service connections, there may be evidence of obsolete services. One such indicator is capped gas outlets on walls or ceilings in homes and apartments (often dating back to the late nineteenth and early twentieth centuries). Coal chutes on the side of a house indicate that the structure was at one time heated with coal, not through gas or electric networks. Any evidence of a privy or outdoor pump similarly indicates that the structure predates the introduction of water and sewer connections.

Sometimes the nonfunctioning system is difficult to decipher. For instance, some entrepreneurs in the late nineteenth century tried to market piped-in refrigeration, heating from a central power source, and pneumatic tubes for sending mail and small packages to homes in communities across North America. While none of these systems took hold in any serious way, they do surface from time to time in historical investigations, and remind us that history is by no means without missteps.

Armed with the physical evidence of service connections, the next move is to time their introduction into a house. The construction date of the home serves as the start. If a house was built before the 1870s, there are likely to have been many additions to the infrastructure connections over time. On the other hand, if a home was built after World War II, it is possible that all, or all but one, infrastructure connections were made at the time of construction.

There are a number of basic sources that can be used in dating infrastructure improvements within an individual structure. Blueprints and building permits often provide information on the service connections made at the time of construction. In some communities, utility billings are readily accessible, and the earliest billing is often the date when householders connected with an infrastructure system. Later building permits may indicate upgrades to infrastructure connections. Sewer and water departments sometimes maintain maps that date the extension of services. Locating a house on such a map provides a rough estimate of the earliest date that a service extension could have been made.

Dating the infrastructure connections for an individual home raises some interesting questions about how individuals lived within homes, and how they were/are connected to the wider community. Households were confronted with the fact that fittings for indoor plumbing or illumination were of no use unless the building they were in was located adjacent to infrastructure systems. Initially, these systems were available only in the inner core of the nation's largest cities. Perhaps at no time was the contrast between urban and rural living so dramatic as in the decades after the Civil War. During those years, infrastructure networks developed in the largest cities in North America. Comparable development in smaller cities and communities did not generally come until the turn of the century. Put plainly, it made a great deal of difference where a home was located when discussing the possibility of service connections. While households in large urban centers were transformed by the presence of service connections, residents of smaller cities, suburbs, and rural areas continued to live in what increasingly was seen as an old-fashioned world.

Of course, the threat of fire was as real in a small community as it was in a large city. While more healthful than crowded city centers, suburban residents were increasingly aware of the connection between impure water and disease. Inadequate and impure water supply and pressure served as important motivations for the development of pub-

While we often take for granted improvements such as paved streets and sidewalks, historical photographs often show how streets looked before these improvements. These images remind us of the changes which public works effect on the
local landscape. Here, an unpaved main street in 1940 Irwin, Iowa, illustrates
what a community looked like in the not too distant past. *Courtesy of the Bureau
of Agricultural Economics, Washington, D.C.*

lic water supplies in many communities. In addition, families sought
water connections so they could install indoor plumbing, just as their
city neighbors were doing.

Residents outside the largest cities had several options for obtaining
these infrastructure connections. They could move to areas that had
these services in place, they could band together to build private systems, or they could petition local governments for services. Local researchers intent on tracing the history of infrastructure systems often
explore the initial residential development and any community associations concerned in service provision, as well as the local governments involved in building infrastructure.

SUGGESTED READINGS

When beginning research on home buildings, consult Barbara J.
Howe, Dolores A. Fleming, Emory L. Kemp, and Ruth Ann Overbeck,

eds., *Houses and Homes: Exploring Their History* (Nashville: American Association for State and Local History, 1987).

Several other books devote attention to infrastructure changes in homes: Ruth Schwartz Cowan, *More Work for Mother: The Ironies of Household Technology from the Open Hearth to the Microwave* (New York: Basic, 1983); Susan Strasser, *Never Done: A History of American Housework* (New York: Pantheon Books, 1982); David P. Handlin, *The American Home: Architecture and Society, 1815–1915* (Boston: Little, Brown, and Co., 1979); Gwendolyn Wright, *Building the American Dream: A Social History of Housing in America* (Cambridge: MIT Press, 1981); and Clifford E. Clark, Jr., *The American Family Home, 1800–1960* (Chapel Hill: The University of North Carolina Press, 1986).

CONCLUSIONS:
THE IMPORTANT
ROLE OF
LOCAL HISTORIANS

Public works history is an exciting subdiscipline within history. Local historians, public works practitioners, public historians, and academics all contribute to research in this field.

Academic historians, who teach and research from their bases in colleges and universities, approach public works from directions as diverse as engineering, urban, political, and social histories. Other academics, including those in political science, public policy, sociology, and law, are actively involved in projects directly related to public works history.

Academic historians are joined by public historians in their professional efforts to further expand our knowledge of history. Many public historians are employed by governmental agencies to document and research past projects and to provide background for current policy questions. On a federal level, public historians interested in public works are employed by agencies that include the U.S. Army Corps of Engineers, the Bureau of Reclamation, the U.S. National Park Service, and the Canadian Parks Service.

In addition, through the efforts of such organizations as the Public Works Historical Society (PWHS), public works professionals participate in researching and writing the history of their own field. Since the foundation of the PWHS in 1976, a regular dialogue between academic and public historians and public works professionals has fostered exciting new directions for research—and application of that research. For instance, the PWHS recently completed a history of the Interstate Highway System sponsored by the American Association of State Highway and Transportation Officials (AASHTO). This project included over one hundred interviews with engineers involved in the Interstate Highway System from the 1950s through the present. Cooperation between these engineers and historians led to the genesis and completion of this unique project.

161

A largely missing component, which would again increase knowledge about public works history, is the active participation of local historians. Their work in exploring the history of utilities and services within a community would expand the field of public works history in several ways.

First, it would move research from the largest cities to small- and medium-sized communities. This would help to provide a far more balanced picture of public services and utilities in the past. Local historians have the tools to provide the evidence needed to answer many questions regarding the development of infrastructure in communities of all sizes, including whether industrialization was as crucial to smaller communities as it was to North America's largest urban areas.

Second, within any community, contact between public works professionals and local historians would allow for cross-fertilization. Public works professionals might suggest research projects which would be of particular interest to them, while local historians could help public works engineers to see the context in which public works history played out within their community.

Third, local historians, with their intimate knowledge of community history, can challenge academic and public historians to explore the invisible history of those who built systems and those who used them. This part of public works history is most accessible within specific communities. The men and women who built public works through their hard labor remain virtually unknown. For public works history to truly provide a rounded picture of the development of utilities and services, researchers must fill in the blanks about these laborers. Local historians can provide particular stories from their communities to serve as building blocks for filling in this hole.

In the same way, academic or public historians have devoted little attention to the ways in which services have transformed everyday life, particularly within individual businesses and households. Local historians can investigate the ways in which these systems affected life for particular families in particular communities—and especially the ways in which women were involved. Again, this information will provide a wider view of the ways in which public works have and will in the future affect our lives.

Interspersed throughout this volume are short biographies of individuals who have made their mark in public works history (for example,

M. M. O'Shaunnessy, Caroline Bartlett Crane, Julius Walker Adams, and Albert E. Berry). Much of this biographical information has been drawn from a monthly column which has appeared in the *APWA Reporter* (published by the American Public Works Association for its members) for seventeen years. Public works professionals, staff members, and historians author these short pieces, which often come from larger research projects.

One very important way in which local historians could contribute to knowledge of public works would be to contribute articles of this sort for publication. The approximately 2,000-word pieces consider individuals important to public works, the only restriction being that they are deceased. For more information, contact the Public Works Historical Society, 106 W. 11th Street, Kansas City, MO 64105-1806.

How can a better knowledge of public works history, coming from the integrated work of academic and public historians, public works professionals, and local historians make a difference?

Infrastructure systems allow us to talk about notions of community through tangible measures such as taxes, special assessments, and private developments. Community is no longer a difficult concept to pin down. Public works historians see it when a group of individuals is willing to bear together the costs of services which will benefit not simply themselves, but others within an area as well.

Because infrastructure networks cannot be constructed without funding and direction, studying their histories can provide insights into political discussion in the past—who had power, who didn't—by looking at who got what services, and who paid for them. Studying infrastructure networks also allows us to see changes in governmental responsibility generally and shifting responsibility between levels of government.

Infrastructure connections provide individuals with basic links to their communities and with the rest of the world. Studying the history of these connections provides us the opportunity to explore the ways in which daily life has changed—or stayed the same—for residents in a community over the course of its history. Services such as water, sewerage, garbage collection, and gas and electric hookups are straightforward ways to examine any changes in the way residents in any community have lived their lives. They also remind us of the ways in which community-wide decisions can profoundly influence the daily lives of individuals.

INDEX